TOP 125
UNUSUAL
THINGS
TO SEE IN ONTARIO

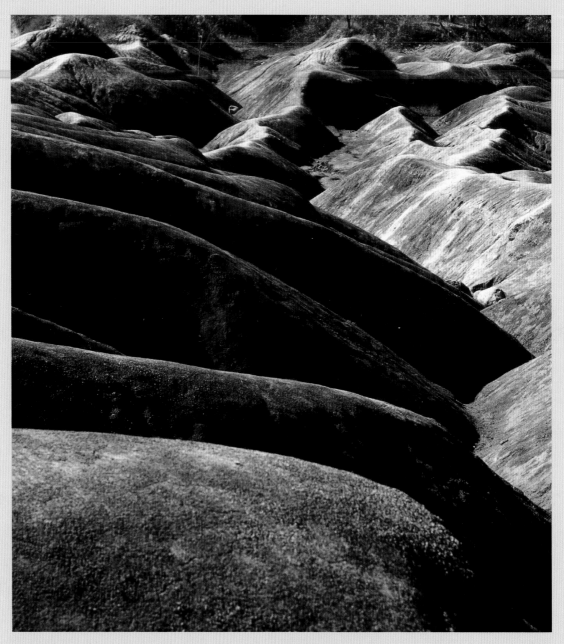

Ontario's painted desert. Medina shale, dramatically exposed,
in a 37-hectare hillside north of the village of Cheltenham. See page 167.

TOP 125
UNUSUAL THINGS
TO SEE IN ONTARIO

RON BROWN

The BOSTON
MILLS PRESS

A BOSTON MILLS PRESS BOOK

Published by Boston Mills Press, 2014

First printing

Publisher Cataloging-in-Publication Data (U.S.)

Brown, Ron, 1945-
   Top 125 unusual things to see in Ontario / Ron Brown.
Related to: Top 100 unusual things to see in Ontario; Toronto, Boston Mills Press, 2007.
[272] p. : col. photos. ; cm.
Includes index.
Summary: A guide to the hidden treasures found in Ontario: a river that disappears, log cabins in the centre of a major city, a high-rise privy, the Canal Museum, ghost towns and more.
ISBN-13: 978-1-77085-423-9 (pbk.)
1. Ontario - Guidebooks. 2. Curiosities and wonders - Ontario Guidebooks. 3. Ontario - Pictorial works. I. Title.
917.1304/5 dc23   F1057.7.B778 2014

Library and Archives Canada Cataloguing in Publication

Brown, Ron, 1945-, author
   Top 125 unusual things to see in Ontario / Ron Brown.
Includes index.
ISBN 978-1-77085-423-9 (pbk.)
   1. Ontario–Guidebooks. 2. Curiosities and wonders–Ontario–Guidebooks. I. Title. II. Title: Top one hundred and twenty-five unusual things to see in Ontario.
FC3057.B78 2014 917.1304'5 C2014-900571-7

Distributed in the United States by
Firefly Books (U.S.) Inc.
P.O. Box 1338, Ellicott Station
Buffalo, New York 14205

Distributed in Canada by
Firefly Books Ltd.
50 Staples Avenue, Unit 1
Richmond Hill, Ontario
L4B 0A7

Cover and interior design: Lind Design
All photographs courtesy of the author, Ron Brown.

Printed in China

The publisher gratefully acknowledges the financial support for our publishing program by the Government of Canada through the Canada Book Fund as administered by the Department of Canadian Heritage.

CONTENTS

Contents

CENTRAL ONTARIO & TORONTO AREA

COTTAGE COUNTRY & NORTHERN ONTARIO

INTRODUCTION

ONTARIO IS FULL of hidden treasure. Down village streets, in city lanes, and along quiet country roads lie its most unusual sights — houses that seem to float, a river that disappears, log cabins in the centre of a major city. All await the curious explorer. Monuments to murders, massacres and mysterious spy camps bring to life the lesser-known aspects of Ontario's hidden heritage.

This book features my pick of Ontario's top 125 unusual things to see. Most of the listings are easy to find and are open to the public.

In this revised and updated edition, the places are grouped into four geographic regions. Maps pinpoint each location within the region.

So head out and discover whichever treasure appeals at the moment. Temples, towers and quirks of nature offer insight into an Ontario that few even know exists. And that's what looking for treasure is all about.

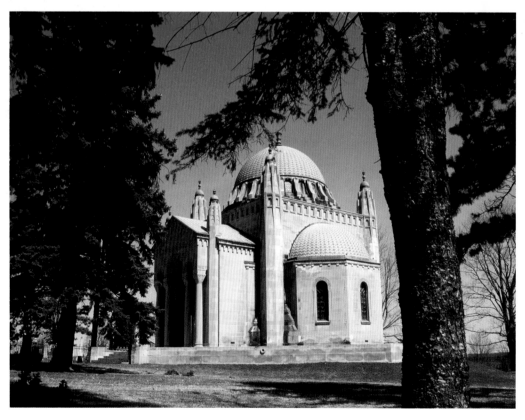

Thomas Foster modelled his memorial to his wife after India's Taj Mahal.
See page 148.

Ouimet Canyon, Ontario's miniature version of the Grand Canyon. See page 228.

EASTERN ONTARIO

N

Renfrew

132

17

22

Ottawa River

Bancroft

41

Ottawa

28

62

24

9

17

Smiths
Falls

Cornwall

10

27

36

25, 26

16

15

15

14

8

3

2

Peterborough

4

21

7

19

401

115

18

Belleville

6

Trenton

7

1

Kingston

Cobourg

33

Map not to scale

Picton

5, 11

13

12, 20, 23

Ontario's "Goat Pastures," or alvars, are unusual areas of thin or nonexistent soil cover, that support rare plant and animal ecosystems.

ONTARIO'S GOAT PASTURES
The Alvar Communities

THEY MAY BE hard to identify at first, and they certainly do not count among Ontario's more spectacular landscapes, but they are one of our most unusual natural features. Indeed, Ontario's alvars are among the most important in North America.

Scientists define alvars as open areas of thin soil over flat limestone or marble rock with little in the way of vegetation. They are, in other words, rock deserts or, as frustrated early farmers derisively called them, "goat pastures."

The Ontario government has moved to protect these unusual areas, as they frequently contain endangered and rare species of plants and animals. They also attract hordes of birdwatchers to witness such species as loggerhead shrikes, upland sandpipers or grasshopper and clay-coloured sparrows.

In Ontario, alvars are found in areas where the limestone bedrock creeps close to the surface — on Manitoulin Island, in eastern Ontario and on the fringes of cottage country east of Lake Simcoe.

Alvars can vary in their appearances. They can look like grasslands, shrublands and even bare limestone.

Unsuspecting pioneer settlers found the unforgiving soils a shock and a disappointment. While the level plains looked promising, the hard limestone beds just a few centimetres beneath the surface broke many a shovel and plough, as well as spirit. Most such farmers would simply take off what lumber they could and move on, leaving stumps sitting on top of the rock. Many logged alvars can still be seen today. In other areas, these farms were gathered into larger units to create shrubby cattle ranches.

In Ontario, alvar landscapes are most striking in an area known as the Carden Plain, located east of Lake Simcoe. Farm roads originally surveyed for the settlers have disappeared or become mere rutted tracks. The Ontario Ministry of Natural Resources has designated the Carden Plain and other alvars as areas of natural and scientific interest (ANSI) and are working with private landowners to preserve these strange habitats. The Carden Plain lies between Kawartha Roads 6 and 36, near Dalrymple.

Other alvars can be found around Napanee, throughout Prince Edward County and on Manitoulin Island.

GHOSTS OF THE GOLD FIELDS

Ontario's Eldorado

THE WORDS "GOLD RUSH" conjure images of Barkerville, B.C., or the Klondike, with their boom-town buildings and barroom brawls. They scarcely evoke thoughts of southern Ontario, in particular the rugged hills north of Belleville.

Yet that is exactly where Ontario's first gold rush took place. It all began in 1866 when court clerk and part-time prospector Marcus Powell discovered a gold-laden cave on the farm of John Richardson. One nugget, he boasted, was the size of a butternut.

Once word got out, the rush was on. Grizzled gold seekers streamed in from as far away as the Cariboo Goldfields in British Columbia. And in the centre of the gold field, the boom town of Eldorado suddenly appeared. A shanty town of eighty buildings on muddy streets, it was as rough and tumble as any of its western counterparts. When sceptical prospectors, led by the notorious Cariboo Cameron, threatened to tear apart some of the mine buildings, twenty-five mounted police were quickly dispatched to keep order.

But they didn't need to stay long, for the gold rush was short-lived. Because the gold was chemically fixed to the parent rock, and impossible to mill using existing techniques, the only profit was through fraud. Disillusioned investors salted the claims with imported gold specimens and sold them to unsuspecting greenhorns.

Finally, about the turn of the century, a new milling process allowed extraction to begin and the overgrown mines sprang back to life. A few mills were erected, and the Central Ontario Railway added a simple wooden station. But even their second life was short, for the gold deposits were smaller than was first thought. After a few years of sputtering activity, the mines fell silent and Eldorado became a ghost town.

Hotels, former stores and even a few of the tiny miners' cabins dot the once-busy network of streets. Of the eighty or so original buildings, only two dozen survive, many with a decidedly boom-town air about them. The structures straddle a 1-kilometre section of Highway 62, a dozen kilometres north of Madoc. Here, a blue historic plaque commemorates Ontario's earliest golden boom town. But high up in the hills above the town, the roofless ruins of the early mills still lie, overgrown and uncelebrated.

2

Eldorado was the site of Ontario's first gold rush.

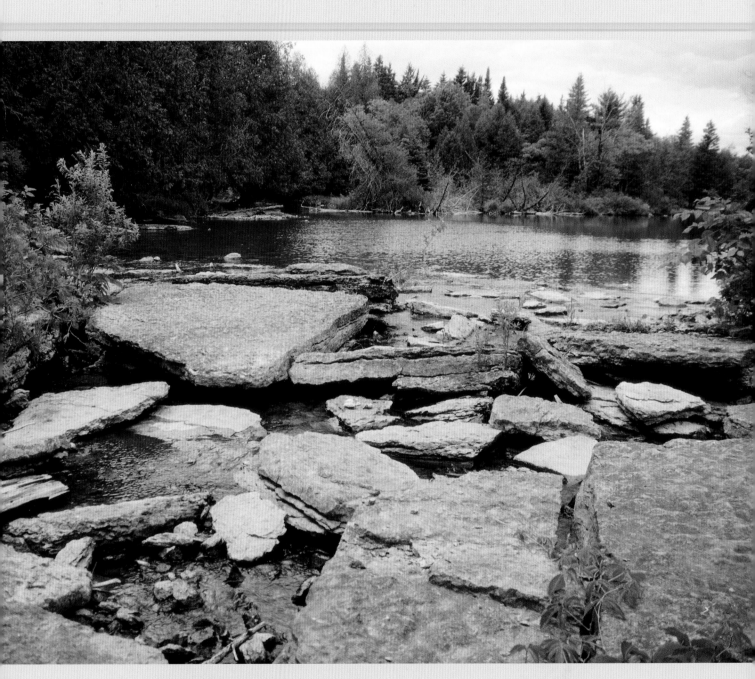

The disappearing Indian River.

THE DISAPPEARING RIVER OF PETERBOROUGH COUNTY

NOW YOU SEE it, now you don't. After flowing wide and swift through the farmland of Peterborough County, the Indian River simply disappears. From its source in Dummer Lake, just south of Stoney Lake, the river meanders southward until, near the village of Warsaw, it enters an area of limestone and vanishes.

Limestone is noted for its solubility in water. Water not only erodes limestone, but can also dissolve it, creating spectacular caves and potholes, known as kettles. But water is also able to seep between the porous layers of limestone and seemingly disappear, and that's just what the Indian River does.

Normally, rivers can flow through an area of limestone and stay in view. The Niagara River does. However, in the vicinity of Warsaw, a large outcrop of porous limestone blocks the flow of the river, and rather than go over or around the rock, the river has found enough cracks to simply flow through it.

From the parking lot in the Warsaw Caves Conservation Area, a path leads past kettles and caves to the river. As you cross the rock fall that blocks the river, you will notice something peculiar — the expanse of fast-flowing water swirls straight toward you and then disappears into the rock beneath your feet. You can hear the strange echoing gurgle of the water as the river makes its way underground. Beyond that point lies the now-dry former river bed, then about a half kilometre downstream the water bubbles back up to the surface to continue its course to Rice Lake.

A popular spot for picnickers, the park also offers a small beach, trails and a network of caves for the cautious explorer. But it is the disappearing river that will provide you with the most vivid memory of this peculiar place.

The Warsaw Caves Conservation Area lies north of Warsaw on County Road 4.

The Royal Canoes in the Canadian Canoe Museum
in Peterborough never had a royal paddler.

A History of Paddling

Peterborough's Canadian Canoe Museum

WHAT COULD BE more Canadian than canoes? And what kind of museum is more "Canadian" than a museum that shows them.

The Peterborough Canoe Museum collection began modestly enough in the 1950s as a private collection assembled by Professor Kirk Wipper at Camp Kandalore, near Minden. As the collection grew, a proper place to store it became necessary, and so appeared the Kanawa Canoe Museum.

But the fleet kept expanding and, by the 1990s, a still larger facility was needed. In 1996, the canoes moved into today's Canadian Canoe Museum in Peterborough. Now housing Canada's largest canoe collection, the museum contains more than six hundred canoes and kayaks.

The museum is laid out as a walk through time. The self-guiding tour leads past examples of dugout canoes, some of them several metres long, and dozens of kayaks that hang from the walls. There's also the freighter canoe, which the fur trade era ushered in, with room for twelve voyageurs and their enormous bundles of fur that could weigh as much as 80 kilograms.

Although it is highly unlikely that royalty ever paddled a canoe (that is, until Prince William and his bride, Catherine, did so on their 2011 visit to Canada), three Royal canoes on display include those given to Queen Elizabeth and Prince Philip and to Prince Charles and Princess Diana, both as wedding gifts. A third Royal canoe was given to Prince Andrew by Lakefield College School as a memento of his school days at that institution. Andrew is now the museum's Royal patron.

But perhaps the most intriguing canoe in the collection is a real silver canoe. This was a gift given in the 1840s to Governor George Simpson by a soldier of the Coldstream Guards out of sheer respect for Simpson's inspirational leadership. Crafted by Garrard's of London, it was acquired by the museum from descendants of Simpson's family.

Visitors to the museum are also likely to see artisans at work carving canoe paddles, or making blankets and boots, or even building a genuine birch bark canoe itself. And don't forget to check out the leather fringed jacket worn by Pierre Trudeau during his carefree paddles in his own canoe.

The Canadian Canoe Museum is on Monaghan Road in Peterborough.

Kingston's Martello Towers provided a flexible
but short-lived line of defence against the Americans.

KINGSTON'S LITTLE ROUND FORTS

FOR ONTARIO'S HISTORY lovers, Kingston is as good as it gets. With its beautiful stone houses and institutional buildings (some dating from the 1790s), its historic forts, and the houses where Canada's first prime minister, Sir John A. Macdonald, slept, the city can keep a history buff occupied for weeks. But the structures that cause the most quizzical looks are the little round forts that seem to be almost everywhere.

Named Martello Towers after their role in repelling an attack at Cape Mortella on Corsica in 1796, these were the last word in defence. Their small size meant that they could be placed in defensive locations otherwise too small for a normal-sized fort. Their circular shape deflected cannon balls, and their high, small windows made them almost impossible to enter. They permitted a flexible line of defence and were almost impregnable.

Of the dozen or so built in Canada (Britain built about two hundred worldwide in the defence of the Empire) half are in Kingston. The oldest were the towers built in Halifax between 1796 and 1798; those in Kingston were added during the 1840s when the Oregon Crisis between Canada and the United States once again raised the spectre of American invasion. But the military usefulness of the forts in Kingston was relatively short-lived, as by 1860, newly introduced naval guns had the capacity to demolish the sturdy bastions with a single shot.

Of Canada's surviving Martello Towers, those in Kingston, with their distinctive roofs and their neat stonework, are considered the most appealing architecturally. All are readily visible. While two are connected to the museum fortress of Fort Henry, two others, the Murney Tower near Macdonald Park and Fort Frederick Tower, are both museums. The one at Fort Frederick was the only tower to be three storeys high, and is part of the Royal Military College. The third pair, those known as Shoal Tower and Cedar Island Tower, lie offshore.

IT CAME FROM OUTER SPACE
The Holleford Meteor Crater

MOST OF US have at one time or another gazed in amazement at the night sky and watched streaks of light. On rare occasions we can hear the crackle as a "close one" burns up in the atmosphere. These are true visitors from outer space — meteors.

About twice a day, somewhere in Canada, a meteor thuds to the Earth. Most are only about 100 grams in weight and make little impact; but a few have struck with a tremendous explosion, ripping apart the ground and leaving telltale circular craters or altered minerals.

To date, scientists have recorded about two dozen meteor craters in Canada. The 95-kilometre-wide strike in Sudbury is Canada's largest. The impact of what must have been an enormous meteor was so broad and deep that it completely altered the mineralization of the bedrock and created Canada's greatest nickel deposit.

Of the five meteor craters in Ontario (others are near Brent in Algonquin Park, at Wanapitei Lake west of Sudbury, and at the Slate Islands in Lake Superior), that at Holleford, north of Kingston, is the most readily visible from the ground. It was first discovered in 1955 by a team of scientists at the Dominion Observatory in Ottawa by poring over aerial photographs. Later research concluded that the extraterrestrial interloper must have arrived around 550 million years ago and measured 90 metres across. Exploding into the ground at an estimated 55,000 kilometres an hour, it has left a crater 2.35 kilometres in diameter and 30 metres deep.

To reach it, drive to Hartington on Highway 38, about 25 kilometres north of Exit 611 on Highway 401. From the centre of the village take the Holleford Road east for about 3 kilometres and follow the road as it bends to the north (left). Another 1.5 kilometres brings you to a T intersection, where you turn right. Then, after another 1.6 kilometres, the road descends a slope. This is the southwest wall of the crater. The road continues east along the slope of the crater for another kilometre to the Crater Farm and the one-time hamlet of Holleford, where a plaque stands by the fence on the north side of the road.

As with most meteor craters in Canada, erosion has softened its features and vegetation covers much of its slope. Yet it is hard not to stand and wonder at how the ground must have shaken when this visitor from outer space thundered to Earth.

6

This crater in the ground occurred when a meteor exploded into the Earth's crust.

TRENTON'S BIG BOULDER

WHILE CLAWING BOULDER after boulder from their fields, many farmers curse the last ice age, claiming bitterly that all they harvested was a new crop of rocks. And they aren't far wrong. For in fields infested with boulders, the freezing and thawing of the ground in the spring in fact squeezes a fresh crop of boulders from beneath the surface.

Most such rocks were deposited during the last ice age, which some scientists claim covered Ontario to a depth of more than a kilometre. As the ice sheets cracked and began to melt about twenty thousand years ago, the torrents of meltwater spewed sand, gravel and rocks into the gaping crevasses. In central Ontario, the ice sheet melted in a long line where the glacial debris formed a ridge of rocky and sandy hills, a bouldery line that stretches from Orangeville in the west to Trenton in east. The deposit is widely known today as the Oak Ridges Moraine.

But it was at Trenton that the ice disgorged its biggest boulder, one the size of a house. Geologists call it the Glen Miller Erratic, their name for boulders that the ice sheets carried far from their parent bedrock. In Glen Miller, the Trenton suburb where it sits, residents simply call it the Bleasdell Boulder.

Its veins of quartz and granite suggest that it has travelled a long distance from its origin in the Canadian Shield far to the north, a testament to the power of the great glaciers. And despite the young forest now surrounding it, the huge stone towers well above the humbled viewer. In fact it contains its own cave, large enough for a person to stand upright. Known now as the Bleasdell Boulder, it is Ontario's largest erratic, measuring 8 metres wide and 7 metres high. Thanks to the efforts of Paul and Maria Heissler, the geologic oddity lies within a conservation area on Highway 33 north of Highway 401.

Trenton's Big Boulder testifies to the awesome power of the glaciers that covered Ontario during the last ice age.

Trains once rambled under the town of Brockville to reach this tunnel.

RAILS UNDER BROCKVILLE
Canada's Oldest Railway Tunnel

THEY SAID, "EVERY railway has to have a tunnel," so the builders of Ontario's earliest railway, the Brockville and Ottawa (B and O), built one.

Until the 1850s, the colonies that would become Canada had relied on muddy pioneer roads and perilous water routes to move people and products. Railways had been operating for two decades in the U.S. and Britain, and in the mid-1850s Canadians decided that it was their turn. Although the Grand Trunk and the Great Western Railway both began operating in Ontario in the 1850s, neither at that time had a tunnel. The B and O Railway was designed to link the St. Lawrence River route with Ottawa and to tap the forests and farms between. And because the town of Brockville was built on a ledge of limestone that cut off the waterfront, the railway engineers decided to blast a tunnel.

Begun in 1854, the tunnel would stretch nearly a kilometre through the limestone mesa. On December 31, 1860, the first wood-burning steam locomotive puffed its way through the darkness, the dim glow from its kerosene headlamp barely illuminating the way. It was Canada's first railway tunnel and the envy of a soon-to-be nation on the verge of the railway era.

But the engineering miracle that was the old Brockville tunnel was later forgotten when, in 1889, the Grand Trunk began digging its 1,800-metre tunnel beneath the St. Clair River to link Sarnia, Ontario, with Port Huron, Michigan. It marked the first time that tunnel builders used compressed air, and the event was featured in newspapers and engineering journals around the world.

Meanwhile, back in Brockville, the engines of the B and O, and later those of the CPR, continued to rumble through the darkness of the old tunnel until use of the passage was discontinued in 1954. A separate spur continued to access the waterfront until 1970.

For many years, Brockville's braver youth would explore the dampened darkness, until the entrance was finally sealed. Today, the tunnel is a historic site controlled by the Brockville museum. Visitors can now venture once more into the tunnel during operating hours and see a nearby CPR caboose.

SMITHS FALLS' HIGH-RISE PRIVY

9

EW OF TODAY'S generation know much of that grand Canadian institution, the outhouse. Yet, for many generations of Canadians, that early-morning trek to the frigid wooden seat was as much a part of everyday life as a warm morning shower is today.

Privies are rare nowadays. But even when they were standard equipment, a two-storey outhouse was almost unheard of, unless you lived in Smiths Falls, Ontario.

In the 1850s, Joshua Bates, a Smiths Falls miller, chose a site next to his Rideau River grist mill to build a house. No ordinary house, it had some unusual features — an indoor brick bake oven, mirror-image facades and an outhouse that was two storeys high.

The logistics of how a two-storey outhouse might function without unpleasant consequences for the lower occupant are not readily apparent. A closer look, however, solves the riddle. Unlike most, this privy is connected to the house itself.

The structure is wide enough that the upper facility need not be located directly above the lower one. In fact, a vertical partition separates the upper facility on one side from the lower facility on the other. While the door to the lower chamber leads directly off the downstairs porch, that to the upper room leads from an upstairs hallway. A simple but effective arrangement, when you think about it.

In 1977 the town purchased the outhouse and the house attached to it and created a museum, restoring it to an 1867 appearance. Now known as the Heritage House Museum, it is located at 11 Old Sly's Road, in the southeast part of Smiths Falls.

While you're in town, be sure to visit the beautifully restored Canadian Northern Railway station at 90 Victoria Street, now a railway museum. More recently, the former Canadian Pacific Railway (CPR) station at 62 Victoria Street has been converted to a community theatre.

At first glance, this two-storey outhouse in Smiths Falls defies logic.

THE RUINS OF ST. RAPHAEL

10

RUINS, ROMANTIC AND picturesque, are associated more with Europe than with North America. Here, ruins tend to be of factories and mills, harsh forms that reflect our obsession with industry rather than beauty. But the ruins of the magnificent St. Raphael Cathedral on County Road 18, 40 kilometres northeast of Cornwall, contain a history, romance and grace that one would more closely identify with Greece or Rome.

In 1764, the revolutionary war in the United States was over, and in return for their loyalty and courage, those who fought for England were rewarded with land grants in what would become Ontario. After trooping wearily behind their commander, Sir John Johnson, the officers and men of the 1st Battalion, King's Royal Regiment of New York (most of Highland Scots origin), finally arrived on the banks of the Raisin River. Here, in eastern Ontario's Charlottenburg Township, their land grants awaited them.

Two years later, five hundred more Scots arrived direct from the Highlands, led by their parish priest, Alexander Macdonnell. The parish grew and prospered. The first father Macdonnell died in 1803 and was replaced by another priest of the same name. The second Father Macdonnell succeeded in making his parish, which he called St. Raphael, the administrative centre of the Catholic Church in Upper Canada.

In 1815 he ordered the building of a large stone church on a hilltop overlooking the farms of his flock. In 1821 the church was consecrated, and when the priest was appointed bishop, the church became a cathedral. It was the largest church in Upper Canada. Five years later he added the Iona Seminary.

For a century and a half, the cathedral dominated the rolling farmlands from its hilltop perch. Then, in 1970, fire roared through the structure. Flames lashed out through the windows, as the roof collapsed in a whirl of sparks. But again the tenacity of their roots came to the fore, bolstered now by the infusion of French-Canadian Catholics, and the parishioners decided the ruins should be neither demolished nor replaced, but rather remain a ruin.

In 1992, a falling stone temporarily closed the site. In 1999 St. Raphael became a National Historic Site, and Friends of St. Raphael Ruins raised $670,000 to stabilize the walls. Once again, visitors may walk through the gates (although weddings are not permitted).

The picturesque ruins of St. Raphael Cathedral.

The Simcoe Island ferry is Ontario's smallest and one of its least-known ferry services.

Ontario's Smallest Ferry

As ontarians hurl their cars along the expressways and toll roads, few pause to consider the more leisurely pace of a ferry ride. Many have tried the popular MS *Chi-Cheemaun*, which swallows 115 cars at a time and glides them across Georgian Bay to and from Manitoulin Island. Few, however, realize that Ontario claims no fewer than sixteen car ferry services, nearly all of them free. Three car ferries cross each of the Ottawa and St. Clair rivers, a pair are for island Native reserves, while Canada's southernmost ferry links mainland Ontario with Pelee Island, Canada's most southerly occupied island. But the greatest concentration of ferries lies near Kingston.

Here, at the entrance to the St. Lawrence River, a handful of large, flat islands attracted early pioneer settlers. Although the populations have subsequently declined, the islands remain occupied, the ferries their lifeline to the mainland.

The largest of the five, the *Wolfe Islander III*, carries more than fifty cars and trucks to busy Wolfe Island. While others link Howe Island and Amherst Island to the mainland, the smallest of them all is the three-car ferry to Simcoe Island. Announced only by a small sign, the landing is nothing more than a beach. Here, the little ferry grinds against the sand and unceremoniously plunks down its gangway. Because it links Simcoe Island only to Wolfe Island, and not to the mainland, the ferry coincides its schedule with that of the *Wolfe Islander III*, or runs as required.

Once home to more than a dozen farm families, Simcoe Island is now more popular for cottaging, and only a pair of farms survive. At the far western end of the limestone island stands the historic Nine-Mile Point Lighthouse. Now automated, the 15-metre tower dates from 1833 and is popular with lighthouse enthusiasts, although it is surrounded by privately owned land. Although it is only one of sixteen ferries that ply Ontario's waters, the Simcoe Island ferry is the smallest, and takes you on an unusual excursion to a place where cars are an anomaly rather than the norm.

THE LAKE ON THE MOUNTAIN

AT FIRST IT looks natural enough — a little lake sparkling in the sun, surrounded by willow trees. But look behind you, and 100 metres below, at the foot of a limestone cliff, spreads Lake Ontario's Bay of Quinte. Then it begins to sink in. The little lake beside you is sitting on the brink of a cliff, with no visible outlet and no visible source.

Located in Prince Edward County, 7 kilometres from the town of Picton, the lake has long puzzled geologists. How did it get there? Why has it stayed there? Until just a few years ago no one even knew how deep it was. Then, as they explored its depths, geologists determined that it was spring fed and about 60 metres deep.

But just as they were solving these puzzles, the scientists uncovered another, even more intriguing mystery. The fluctuations in the water level of the lake seemed to coincide with those occurring in Lake Erie, more than 100 kilometres away and with no direct connection.

Its origins, too, have defied explanation. While most theories involving glacial whirlpools, meteors and volcanoes have been dismissed, the one most commonly accepted involves the collapse of a massive limestone cave beneath the surface. The early Indians believed it was the lake of the gods, and called it Onokenoga.

The attractions around the lake are numerous and don't have a lot to do with its mysteries. A small provincial park beside the lake provides picnicking and hiking, while across the road a lofty viewpoint offers vistas of the Bay of Quinte, the mainland shore, and the free Glenora ferries that shuttle back and forth carrying Highway 33 traffic.

Van Alstine's stone store, which dates from the days of the Loyalists, sits beside the park, while at the foot of the cliff the several buildings that comprise the Glenora mill complex are among the oldest stone mill buildings in the province. But all attention focuses upon the Lake on the Mountain. It has been a mystery since it was discovered, and it will likely remain a mystery for some time to come.

12

Picton's mysterious Lake on the Mountain lurks near the lip
of the cliff that overlooks the Glenora mill.

Dunes at West Lake.

THE DUNE THAT ATE A TOWN

ALTHOUGH IT DIDN'T exactly "eat" a town, a giant wall of sand did move across Prince Edward County between 1890 and 1920 to consume a sizeable settlement. And it was all due to beer.

When the U.S. government slapped a surtax on whiskey during the Civil War, American consumers switched to beer. And the best barley for beer was considered to be Canadian. Canadian farmers hurriedly turned all available fields to barley production. But Prince Edward County, with its mild climate and close proximity to U.S. ports just across Lake Ontario, became Ontario's major barley exporter. Cattle were hustled off their pastures and onto the most marginal lands in the county, the dunes.

Following the retreat of the last glaciers, the Prince Edward Peninsula built up a long beach of sand. Over the centuries the prevailing winds whipped the sand into a ridge of dunes that measured 8 kilometres long, 2 kilometres wide and 50 metres high. Over time, a matte of grasses and shrubs had stabilized the dunes. But once the cattle started to roam them, eating the fragile cover, the dunes grew restless and started once more to move.

Slowly at first, then with increasing determination, the dunes moved inland. Fields, fences and then outbuildings and barns soon disappeared under the moving yellow wall. The West Bay Road had to be realigned a number of times to avoid being consumed. The advancing dunes spared nothing. A brick factory stood stubbornly in the way of the dunes until wind-whipped sand finally forced the owners to dismantle the plant and flee.

Desperate, the farmers planted willows on the dunes, but those had little effect. Finally, after the First World War had ended, a reluctant Ontario government established a tree nursery on them. As roots and branches grabbed the blowing sand the dunes' advances slowed, but they haven't stopped.

Today, on the south shore of West Lake, both in and near the popular Sandbanks Provincial Park, you can see the advancing dunes. Cedar trees, once buried and now exposed, show double sets of roots, while relics of the pioneer brick factory still litter its ill-fated site. Although the dunes no longer advance across the countryside, the winds continue to whip the sand into West Lake. Eventually, the dunes that ate a sizeable settlement will claim the lake and turn it into little more than a pond. Their appetite is insatiable.

The dunes form the backbone of Sandbanks Provincial Park and lie on County Road 12, about 10 kilometres southwest of the village of Bloomfield.

WATERWAY FROM THE PAST

14

The Rideau Canal

IN 1826, THE Duke of Wellington's mind looked to Upper Canada, where memories of the 1812 war with the Americans were still fresh. Wary that the major transportation corridor, the St. Lawrence, lay on the U.S. border, Wellington proposed a canal that would link Kingston, on Lake Ontario, with Wright's Town (now Gatineau), then a small sawmill village on the north side of the Ottawa River, a remote location.

To carry out the difficult job he coaxed Colonel John By out of retirement. For five years, two thousand men sweated in malarial swamplands, hacking bush, trenching channels, and hauling huge limestone blocks for the fifty dams and forty-seven locks. The estimated death rate from malaria was more than 50 percent.

In 1832, By's 200-kilometre waterway opened for traffic, a remarkable feat given the remoteness and total lack of mechanical assistance. A small sawmill town sprang up at the canal's eastern terminus and was named Bytown, after the canal's builder. But By did not return home a hero. Instead, he was court-martialled for allowing his £577,000 budget to swell to more than £870,000.

The canal would provide a key commercial link for the many little mill towns along its path. Then, with the arrival of the railway, its use faded, not rising again until the 1950s and '60s, when the popularity of recreational boating boomed. In 1932, the federal government proposed closing the historic waterway. It was saved only by its role as a vital water-control system.

The canal is famed not just for its pleasure-boating, but for the fact that it remains historically intact, right down to the hand operation of its locks and swing bridges. In fact, in a rare gesture of heritage preservation, the federal government placed the canal's operation in the hands of Parks Canada and has identified the route as a historical monument. In June 2007, UNESCO added the Rideau Canal to its list of World Heritage Sites, one of the first such waterways to be so named.

By's military blockhouses still stand at Kingston Mills, Newboro and Merrickville. At Jones Falls are a triple set of locks, a one-time powder magazine and the world's highest stone dam of its day. The Scottish stonemasons who toiled to construct the stone walls and locks have also left a lasting legacy in the beautiful stone stores and homes of Perth, Merrickville and Kingston. Colonel By may have died a broken man, but even he would have been astonished at the durability of his legacy.

UNESCO has now declared the canal and Kingston's fortress as a World Heritage Site.

THE TEACHING ROCKS 15

Peterborough's Petroglyphs

THE HOLLOW ECHO of water gurgling beneath the rocks at their feet made the two young geologists uneasy. There, in the stillness of the forest north of Stony Lake, they felt as though they had entered a hallowed place. As they swept away the moss from the white crystalline rocks, something caught their eye. Something odd. The surface of the rock was not smooth, as it should have been. Rather, it contained strange etchings, more than nine hundred of them. Although they did not know it on that day in May 1954, the two men had uncovered one of North America's largest and most mysterious Native petroglyphs, the Teaching Rocks.

Like the Christian Bible, the Teaching Rocks tell the Aboriginal story of life. As each young male entered adolescence, the elders of the tribe would lead him to the site, guided by the sound of waterfalls and special guide rocks. One lesson at a time, the elders taught the youngsters the meaning of life, as the Ojibway understood it and as the Teaching Rocks revealed it. The medicine wheel told them that life began as the sunrise in the east. Midday represented midlife, and the west meant old age, while the north referred to the afterlife. The spirits portrayed in the carvings taught that man must coexist with nature.

After each lesson finished, the elders would cover the stones with moss to preserve the carvings from erosion. In 1976, the site, sacred to the First Nations, became a provincial park under the cooperative stewardship of the Curve Lake First Nation. A decade later, to protect the surface from the elements, a glass enclosure was added.

The site is located 55 kilometres northeast of Peterborough, near Highway 28. Here, you wonder at the strange shapes and possibly apply your own interpretations. Then you can watch the Ministry of Natural Resources' award-winning twenty-minute film, *The Teaching Rocks*. Prepared by Lloyd Walton, the film reveals the mysteries as told and narrated by the Ojibway themselves. As you walk back to your car through the woods, you look around you and see nature through different eyes, those of its original stewards.

The mysteries of the Native etchings in Petroglyph Provincial Park have been solved in an award-winning movie, *The Teaching Rocks*, produced by Ontario's Ministry of Natural Resources.

BOATS IN THE AIR
The Kirkfield Lift Lock

SNAKING THROUGH THE middle of Ontario is a water highway, a chain of lakes linked by short streams that connect Lake Ontario on the east and Georgian Bay on the west. Its name is familiar to most Ontarians as the Trent-Severn Waterway. To Ontario's early pioneers it was their lifeline—their only highway. Along its lakes, especially the Kawarthas, they floated out their logs, took their wheat to the mill and travelled for their food.

Although the isolated settlers cried for canals to link the lakes and rivers as early as the 1820s, governments did not act until 1842, when the first lock was constructed at Bobcaygeon. By 1892 a system of locks and canals was nearly complete. But at Peterborough and Kirkfield the level of the water fell so sharply that four costly and water-consuming locks would be required at each location. For a solution, the engineers at Montreal's Dominion Bridge Company, contractor for the canal, looked to an insignificant village in England named Weaver Creek.

There, the locks on the canal were operated by an unusual system known as hydraulic lift locks. Two watertight boxes, each big enough to hold a boat, were balanced hydraulically side by side. As the upper box filled, it became heavier than the lower box and descended, forcing the lower box to the upper level as the lower box opened to release the cargo. This in turn made the lower container lighter and the positions changed. Savings over traditional locks both in time and construction costs, and especially in water usage, were enormous.

Built between 1896 and 1907, two such lift locks groaned into operation at Peterborough and Kirkfield, as Ontario watched in awe. The larger of the two, at Peterborough, looms 20 metres in the air, while that at Kirkfield measures about 17 metres. Each lock contains 1,500 tonnes of water. The two remain the largest in the world, and are the only examples of their kind in North America.

But they were too late to help the settlers. By then the countless little railway companies had created a dense network of railway lines that made water transportation obsolete.

Today, recreation remains the sole function of the Trent Canal and its lift locks. To reflect this emphasis, the whole Trent Canal system is run by the federal department responsible for recreation, Parks Canada. Even for landlubbers the sight of a bucket of boats high in the air has become a tourist attraction in its own right. The lock at Kirkfield is accessible by following signs north from Highway 48 in that village, while that in Peterborough is found by following signs from Highway 28.

16

"There's a boat over your head." The great lift locks at Peterborough and Kirkfield are the only pair of their kind in North America.

THE LOST SETTLEMENT OF NEWFOUNDOUT

THE BLACK DONALD HILLS of eastern Ontario are among the highest mountains in the province. Views from their lofty and windswept summits extend across the wide sweep of the Ottawa Valley to the far Laurentian Mountains in Quebec. Atop this plateau, rugged hills and monstrous boulders were an unpleasant greeting to settlers who, in the 1860s, had trudged up the Opeongo Colonization Road to seek their prized farm lots.

At various intervals, sideroads crept up the steep hillsides from the busy settlement road. Near Plaunts Mountain, another sideroad led to yet another tract of land. Here more than a dozen farm families hauled their worldly goods up the narrowing trail and began to carve out their farms. They named their isolated little world Newfoundout.

The settlers built their crude shanties and barns out of the plentiful logs. Apple trees were planted, and sheep and chickens wandered the yards. Cattle grazed in the rocky pastures. Any hopes of growing crops, however, were quickly dashed by the stony soil and numerous boulders, many the size of a small house.

Amenities were few. While some farmers sawed logs or performed blacksmithing, there were no stores, schools or churches. But the distance and the hardship and the sterility of the farmland gradually took their toll, and one by one the families packed their belongings and went back down the mountain. By 1950, Newfoundout was completely abandoned. It had become a lost settlement.

The narrow trail still winds through the trees and up the steep mountainside, but above the slope, empty barns and roofless cabins abound. Rusting cars and shattered farm equipment litter the overgrown pastures. More distant farmers often log the area or graze their cattle, but Newfoundout has no human inhabitants. It does, however, have a spiritual one.

Sometime around the turn of the twentieth century, one Sylvester Briggs was urging his team up the steep and narrow roads of Plaunts Mountain. Suddenly a tree crashed into his horses, sending his wagon careening back down the mountain. As it plunged over the side, the wagon crushed Briggs' leg, leaving the unfortunate teamster—unable to walk or drag himself home—to starve to death. His body was found two years later. Even today, local residents will gladly regale the listener with accounts of Briggs still calling out on that lonely, dark mountain for help that never came.

Newfoundout extends along Newfoundout Road, south of Opeongo Road and west of Highway 41.

A plateau atop in the Black Donald Hills, which hide the ruins of Newfoundout.

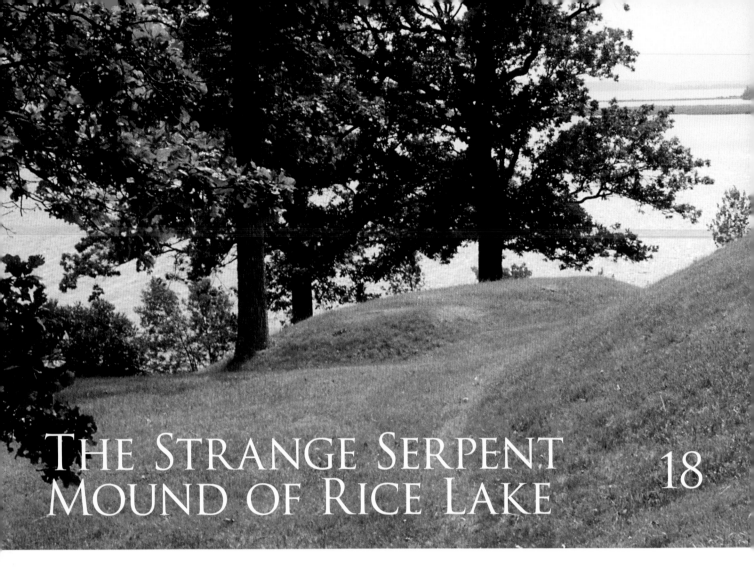

THE STRANGE SERPENT MOUND OF RICE LAKE

IRONICALLY, THE STRONGEST visual evidence of Ontario's Native heritage deals not with life, but with death. Usually, places where Ontario's early peoples lived are seldom discernible to any but the trained archaeologist. Yet where they died can leave prominent physical features.

Take, for example, Rice Lake's unusual serpent mound. Although no other such mounds exist elsewhere in Canada, burial mounds in the shape of giant snakes are common in the Ohio Valley of the United States.

The mound on the north shore of Rice Lake is 2 metres high, 8 metres wide, and a twisting 60 metres long. Several other burial mounds, in the more common oval shapes, surround it. An example of the latter also exists at Taber Hill Park in Scarborough, uncovered when the site was being prepared for housing. Archaeologists can't decide whether the serpent mound was intended to resemble a snake, since it lacks a "head," or was an ordinary burial mound that was somehow extended.

Following the retreat of the glaciers around twelve thousand years ago, the Arctic-like area abounded in caribou, bison and possibly even mammoths. The first inhabitants were nomadic. As the climate warmed, forests covered the tundra, bringing smaller game like deer and rabbits. Berries and root crops became part of the staple diet. The time of the nomads was about to end.

Around 1000 BC, the mound-building culture entered the area. Originating in the Ohio Valley, it gradually made its way into Ontario, culminating in the collection of

The Rice Lake area offers Canada's greatest concentration of tear-shaped glacial hills known as "drumlins." The Serpent Mounds (closed at this writing) were built amid the drumlin field. (Thanks to Elmhirst's Resort on Rice Lake for kind research assistance on that scenic area.)

mounds on Rice Lake. No evidence suggests that this was a village site. The absence of bones from winter game indicates that it was, rather, a summer gathering place for trading, rice harvesting and burials.

Around AD 500 a revolutionary new way of life arrived. Corn and squash replaced hunting and gathering. Permanent villages were built, with longhouses surrounded by palisades. Pits, instead of mounds, were used for burials. The presence of burial pits just north of the mounds, and a habitation area west of them, confirms the existence of the new lifestyle. Consecutive harvests eventually leached the soil, and the inhabitants moved to more fertile grounds.

The arrival of the Europeans in the late eighteenth and early nineteenth centuries ended that way of life, as First Nations peoples were moved onto reserves. A logging dam near the outlet to Rice Lake flooded the rice beds, and a way of life ended forever. Today, the mounds are part of Serpent Mounds Park, where a long-vanished culture and custom can be interpreted by a modern world.

Lying at the end of Serpent Mounds Road south of Keene, the park and campground are administered by the Hiawatha First Nation.

THE HELL HOLES OF EASTERN ONTARIO 19

A WALK THROUGH THE forest can sometimes be a dangerous thing, not necessarily from wolves or bears or even deer hunters, but from a careless step into a hole, especially when the hole leads to Hell.

The limestone ridge along the Salmon River north of Napanee contains some of the area's most unusual natural features. There are caves, crevices and odd-looking rock columns. But the strangest of the oddities are what locals call the "Hell Holes."

To early settlers unfamiliar with geology, these holes in the forest floor seemed to have no end. While most are little larger than foxholes, a few are large enough to allow a human to squeeze through. Those who braved the descent found caverns that stretched in many directions.

Geologists refer to these phenomena as "karst" features. Karst topography occurs when soft limestone layers beneath a hard upper layer dissolve in water. This weathering causes caves and caverns, and the Hell Holes. Similar to caves, the holes in the forest floor can open into large, pitch-black rooms, one of which was once large enough to hold twenty people (it later collapsed). While there are other locations in Ontario with similar features, the ridge by the Salmon River, near the village of Roblindale, offers the greatest concentration of these cavities.

Most are located in the privately run Hell Holes Park. Here, a self-guided trail, a little over 3 kilometres long, leads not only to the strange holes, but also over natural rock bridges, through eerie canyons lined with layered cliffs and columns, and then to the Devil's Horses' Stable hole, 7.5 metres deep and 2.5 by 3.5 metres square. A ladder leads to those depths.

Hell Holes Park is located on Centreville Road about 5.5 kilometres east of Highway 41, and 10.7 kilometres north of Highway 401 (Exit 579). Snacks, gifts and, of course, flashlights are available in the log cabin shop. It is said that one visitor even took his wedding vows in the Hell Holes. The duration of this marriage is not known.

Early pioneers thought that these bottomless pits led straight to Hell.

WARTIME GHOSTS
Camp Picton

A VISIT TO THE top of the cliff that overlooks the attractive lakeside town of Picton reveals more than just a stunning view of the town below. It also unveils an intact collection of abandoned air base buildings — hangars, barracks and officers' apartments. Unlike most remaining World War II military buildings, these are all covered with wood-shingle siding.

The base was established in 1938 and became an air-training facility in 1940, when most of the buildings were constructed. At its peak, the base housed forty-five officers and eight hundred rank and file. From the seven hangars, planes took off to practise on the nearby bombing ranges while gunnery practice took place to the south of the camp.

In late 1944, the gunnery and bombing training ended, and the camp was turned over to the RCAF, which operated it as an equipment-maintenance facility.

At the beginning, relations with the population of Picton were rocky, and complaints of drunkenness, rowdyism and venereal disease flooded the commander's office.

After the war ended, the base became a training centre with new facilities that included a post office, skeet range and theatre, as well sporting facilities for badminton, basketball, floor hockey and archery.

In 1960, the base changed roles once again, becoming and remaining an operational base until 1969, when all military operations there ceased, and the base was abandoned.

Now privately owned and known as Loch Sloy Industrial Park, the few buildings in use house small industries and a fire department, while air cadets and a flying club use a number of the hangars.

But the overall appearance remains that of a massive ghost town. Rows of wood-shingled barracks stand along weed-strewn roads, playing fields lie overgrown, and the two-storey officers' apartments look out on shrubby lawns. So authentic does the facility feel that in 1993, the CBC used it as a location in its made-for-TV movie *Dieppe*. The site, much of which is behind a chain-link fence, lies along Mountain Road on the south side of Picton.

To reach this ghostly sight, follow Church Street south from the centre of Picton.

20

Rows of barracks line the weedy street in the abandoned air base overlooking Picton.

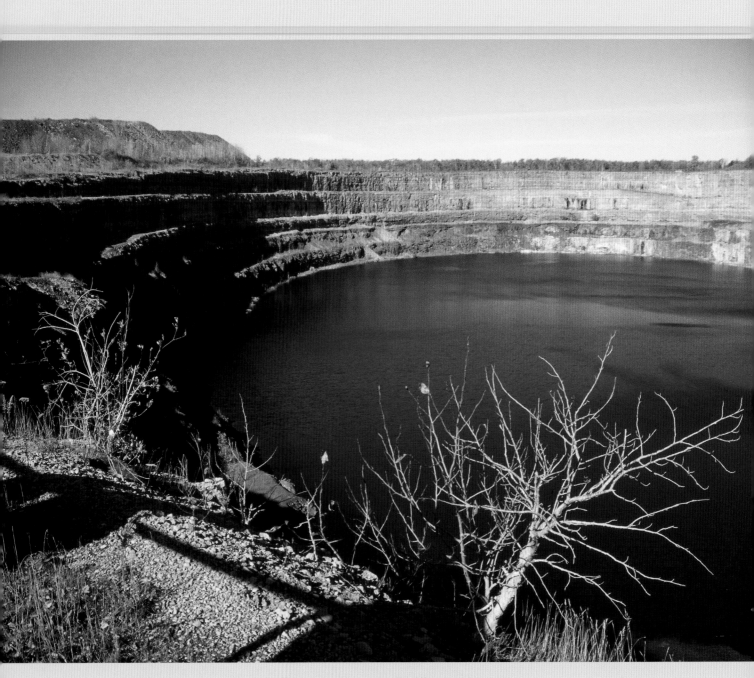

This mammoth open pit at Marmora is gradually filling with water.

Marmora's Big Hole

THE HUGE PIT may ultimately become Ontario's biggest pool. For as each year passes the gaping cavity left by the Marmoraton Iron Mine fills with a little more water. Though nobody will be swimming in it any day soon, it makes for one of Ontario's most unusual mining sights.

Mining days in Marmora date back to 1820. An iron magnate named Charles Hayes hacked a trail through the dark forests of central Hastings, hundreds of kilometres from the nearest city of any size. Here he began the construction of a mine, mill and smelter for the production of iron. The community of Marmora quickly grew to a population of two hundred.

For a time, Marmora and its neighbour, Blairton, now a ghost town, were the leading iron producers in the country. Difficulty in transporting the iron out, however, proved their undoing. When canals were completed along the St. Lawrence River, cheaper iron could be imported, and Marmora's iron-mining days were over. Almost.

In 1949 an aeromagnetic survey revealed strange magnetic anomalies east of the town. Drilling quickly followed, revealing an immense body of ore, 700 metres long and 150 metres deep. The only problem was the 45 metres of limestone that lay on top of it.

In 1951, Bethlehem Steel Company began to haul away the intervening rock, and was soon removing a million tonnes of magnetic ore every year. Canadian National Railway trains carried it to the company's plant in Lackawanna, New York, where it was concentrated and pelletized. By the late 1970s the ore supply was exhausted, leaving a massive circular pit a third of a kilometre across and fully 200 metres deep.

During the mine's operation, a viewing area was provided so that the public could watch the monster trucks grind up out of the gaping hole, loaded with ore. Although the mine no longer operates, the viewing area reveals the emerging lake. The road to the viewing area leads south of Highway 7, just 1.4 kilometres east of the traffic lights in Marmora. Marmora's original iron smelter site is now marked by a plaque in a small park near the downtown area.

22

With its five stone arches, the Pakenham Bridge
is the only one of its kind in North America.

PAKENHAM'S STONE ARCH BRIDGE
North America's Longest

AMONG ONTARIO'S HERITAGE features, bridges are the least appreciated; yet Ontario boasts many distinctive bridges. For example, West Montrose, near Kitchener, is the only remaining covered bridge in Ontario; and a railway swing bridge provides the only road access to Manitoulin, the world's largest freshwater island. One of the most beautiful of Ontario's bridges is Pakenham's bridge, the only five-span stone arch bridge in North America.

Built in 1901, it replaced a rickety wooden structure. The old bridge was so unsafe that it was illegal to cross "at a faster pace than a walk." Designed by the firm of O'Toole and Keating, the new 85-metre bridge is made up of five 25-metre stone arches on piers that are 3 metres thick. The huge stones for the bridge were dragged from a nearby quarry. The largest stone is 3 metres long by nearly a metre square, and weighs 5 tonnes.

In 1984, Ontario's Ministry of Transportation, along with the Ontario Heritage Foundation and Ottawa's National Capital Commission, restored the bridge, inserting reinforced concrete into the deck and parapet walls in the stonework. Framed by its wooded limestone shoreline, the bridge is a popular subject for photographers and artists.

Pakenham village itself is also worth a visit. Despite its location, well inland from Ontario's first towns and villages, Pakenham got off to an early start. By 1831 it had become the site of a sawmill, store and post office, and was named Little Falls. In 1840, Andrew Dickson sold the first village lots, and just twenty years later the village claimed a population of eight hundred. Despite getting the railway in the 1880s, Pakenham failed to grow, and the population is about the same today, which has helped preserve its rich heritage.

On the main street, only a short distance from the bridge, are businesses such as Byrne House Hardware, housed in a mid-1800s Classical Revival building; Paddye Mann Designs in an 1830s stone building; and Ontario's "oldest" general store. Built in 1840, Pakenham's general store contains crafts, memorabilia and freshly baked breads, as well as the usual range of grocery items. On the opposite side of the bridge, the Stone Bridge Shop operates from a converted 1842 gristmill.

Pakenham is on Highway 15 about halfway between Almonte and Arnprior, and about 60 kilometres west of downtown Ottawa. Caution should be used if crossing the bridge on foot; there is no sidewalk, the roadway is narrow and County Road 20 can be busy.

A City for the Birds   23
Picton's Birdhouse City

I N THE SHADOW of a cliff near Picton, Ontario, there lies a city that is strictly for the birds. Started in 1978 by the Prince Edward Region Conservation Authority, Birdhouse City is a collection of more than eighty birdhouses. Not just any birdhouses, they have been designed to copy many of the area's actual buildings. The city is the legacy of former authority superintendent Doug Harnes, whose skill in woodworking led to the creation of this bird city's first structures.

The first to be built was a re-creation of the Massasauga Park Hotel. Measuring more than 1.5 metres square, it was supported by two poles and boasted three thousand miniature shingles. Pretty soon everyone got into the act, and birdhouses of all descriptions began to show up. Participants in Experience '80 contributed a paddle wheeler, a police car and a "fly-in" theatre, while the local McDonald's donated, naturally, a McDonald's "fly-through."

Visitors arrive, often by the busload, to see a Greek temple, a Pennsylvania Dutch barn, and Picton's historic Crystal Palace, while the "departed" can find comfort in the "Nest In Peace" Funeral Home.

Nor was city planning overlooked. The architectural drafting class of Prince Edward Collegiate planned the city with streets like Finch Avenue and Swallow Drive. The Lake Ontario Cement Company donated labour and material for a central fountain.

Sadly, due to financial constraints, many of the structures have seen maintenance slip, and several need repair and repainting. Still, birds love it. The purple martins, the wrens and the bluebirds flit from cottage to carousel to the Thrush Bank. When winter comes, however, most of the residents become "snow birds."

Birdhouse City is in the Macaulay Mountain Conservation Area on County Road 8.

"Empty nesters" in Picton's Birdhouse City.

CANADA'S GIBRALTAR
Bon Echo Rock

GLOWING GOLD AND red in the rays of the evening sunset, and framed by pine and birch trees, Bon Echo Rock is a ready-made subject for a painting or a photograph. Rising from a geological fault line for 1.6 kilometres along Mazinaw Lake, this 91-metre cliff has acquired the nickname "Canada's Gibraltar."

Its appeal dates back a long time. For centuries, Native canoists paused at the foot of the sheer rock face and, using ochre and bear grease, painted their impression of the life they lived and the creatures they revered. These birds, mammals and even human figures are still portrayed in what is considered Ontario's largest-known collection of pictographs.

The place also appealed to Flora MacDonald Denison. In 1919, Denison, one of Ontario's earliest women's-rights advocates, bought the Bon Echo Inn. She transformed the resort into a retreat for Canadian artists and formed the Walt Whitman Club of Bon Echo. For many years the haven drew such artists as Group of Seven painter Frank Johnston, who sketched the cover of Denison's literary magazine, the *Sunset of Bon Echo*.

Following Whitman's death in 1919, Flora Denison added what has become the rock's most unusual feature—a tribute to the poet carved into the rock face. In letters a foot high are the words from his poem "Leaves of Grass."

My foothold is tendon'd and mortised in granite
I laugh at what you call dissolution,
and I know amplitude of time.

The tribute is visible only from the water and is just north of the narrows that divide Upper and Lower Mazinaw Lake.

Bon Echo Provincial Park was created in 1959 after Flora Denison's son Merrill, English Canada's first important twentieth-century playwright, turned the site over to the Ontario government. It is eastern Ontario's largest provincial park.

Casual campers can drive to one of the more than five hundred campsites, while those seeking seclusion can canoe or hike to more remote locations. While rock climbers scale or rappel the sheer granite face, the more passive among us are content to simply stand at the narrows and paint, take photographs or just try out the echo of Canada's Gibraltar.

The park lies on Highway 41, about 40 kilometres north of Highway 7 at Kaladar.

24

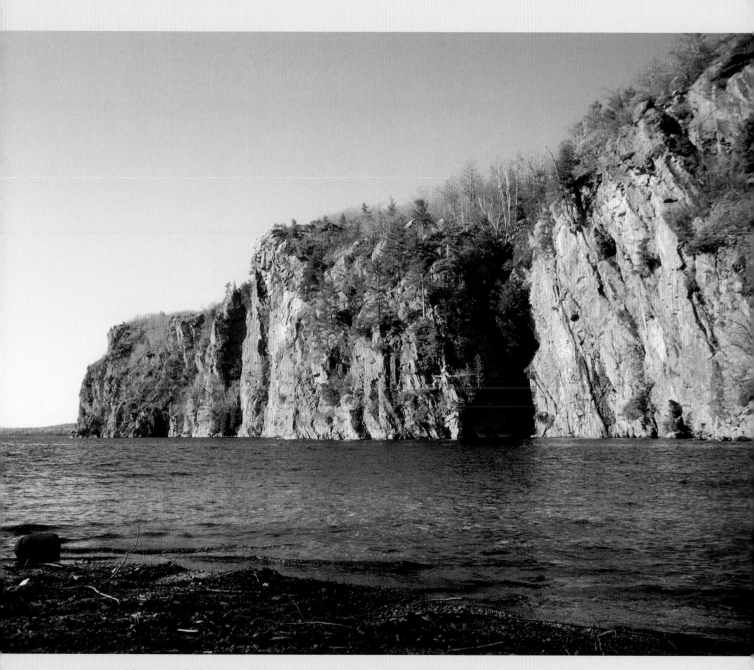

The remarkable Bon Echo Rock has been dubbed "Canada's Gibraltar."

The historic carousel in Roseneath is Canada's oldest country carousel.

'Round and 'Round We Go

The Roseneath Carousel

A SMALL FAIRGROUND IN a tiny Ontario village is probably the least likely place to find one of Ontario's most historic amusement rides, and that is the hundred-year-old carousel in the village of Roseneath located just east of Rice Lake.

Hidden within a large, circular, orange-coloured shed, the carousel was built in Abilene, Kansas, in 1906 — a time before TVs and computer games, when amusement parks and fairgrounds were common sources of recreation.

By 1932, the carousel with its forty bass-wood horses and two wooden boats had made their way to Mohawk Park beside a tram line in Brantford, Ontario, where it languished. In that year, the rail line closed and the ride was placed in storage. The head of the Roseneath Agricultural Society heard about the hidden treasure, and for $675 purchased it and moved it to the Roseneath fairgrounds. To protect the find from the elements, the society erected a sixteen-sided wooden shed. By 1986, with the carousel in dire need of refurbishing,

a fundraising campaign was launched. Horses had to be painstakingly repainted in the same colours as the originals, while some parts were re-carved. Much of this exacting labour was done by master carver Konstantin von Waldburg.

Unfortunately, the sixteen screen panels in the centre of the carousel had become so fragile they could not be restored. New panels commemorating local scenes now rest in their places, most them the work of local artist Ron Bolt.

Thanks to $400,000 in donations and much volunteer labour, the historic merry-go-round was back in business by 1995.

Although the "gold rings" have long since vanished, music plays from a genuine 1934 Wurlitzer pipe organ with actual paper scrolls. The tunes today are likely to be "Rock Around the Clock" or "Locomotion."

Ontario does possess another heritage carousel, that in Port Dalhousie. Although the latter is considered to be a Coney Island–style ride, the one in Roseneath falls into the country fair category and is said to be the only such structure in Canada.

THE SYMBOLIC CENOTAPH 26

Alderville First Nation

Most ontario communities contain memorials to honour members who have served and died defending Canada in time of war. Most date from the end of the First World War and are usually simple plaques, while others offer more elaborate statuary. But the cenotaph that rises above the First Nations community of Alderville near Rice Lake seems at first to be a puzzling agglomeration of cubes, orbs, pillars and chains.

As with much in First Nations culture, the Alderville Cenotaph is highly symbolic. The large cube that surmounts the 18-metre-high white structure represents the four corners of the Earth. The three globes symbolize the Holy Trinity, and the three pillars the three holy virtues of faith, hope and charity.

All are mounted on a square base, its sides representing the four freedoms for which those remembered fought: freedom of speech, freedom of religion, freedom of the press and freedom from fear.

Nine smaller cubes are for those Alderville Natives who perished in the First World War, and the thirty-five links honour those who served. The concrete structure rises 18 metres and was the first in Canada to commemorate the contribution and sacrifice of Canada's First Nations peoples during the First World War. Subsequent plaques commemorate those who served in the Second World War and the Korean War.

The cenotaph was designed in 1927 by Alf and Clarence McKeel and constructed by local volunteers.

The 300 residents of the community are of the Ojibwa First Nations, relocated here from the Bay of Quinte around 1830. An additional thousand band members live off the reserve.

The band also administers the nearby rare Black Oak Savannah, a remnant landscape of tall grass prairie and scattered black oak. It was designated by the band council in 2000 as a Natural Heritage Site.

The First Nations cenotaph at Alderville was the first in Canada to honour First Nations' service in World War One.

27

The "Adam and Eve" boulders in Buckhorn have become a local attraction.

BUCKHORN
Ontario's "Boulder City"

UNLIKE ITS MORE famous American cousins (Boulder City, Colorado; Boulder City, Nevada), Buckhorn is an attractive canal-side hamlet scenically situated where the waters of Pigeon Lake flow through the lock of the Trent Canal into those of Buckhorn Lake. It is one of cottage country's more scenic locations, where the brilliant pink rock outcrops of the Canadian Shield seemingly glow in the bright sunshine.

But Buckhorn also offers one of the area's most extensive fields of pink boulders. Most of these globes range in size from a grapefruit to a beach ball. There are a few, however, that stand out for their unusual size; these are the "Adam and Eve" rocks and the "Teetering" rock.

Geologists call rocks such as these "erratics" and have labelled Buckhorn Ontario's "erratic capital." Some twenty thousand years ago, the vast ice sheets that crept across the province wrenched these stones from the surface and carried them perhaps several kilometres, or even just a few metres.

Looming more than 5 metres above a granite floor, the "Adam and Eve" boulders stand like twins in a forest opening on a ridge above the aptly named "Adam and Eve Road." Sitting on a parcel of land donated to the municipality in 1963 by the Charles Jones family and maintained by Buckhorn Sand and Gravel, they have become a minor local attraction. From a small roadside parking area, steps lead to a commemorative plaque that helps visitors appreciate this unusual geological feature.

On the south side of the Buckhorn lock, visible beside Highway 23, stands the "Teetering" rock — so named because the 5-metre-high erratic rests on a base so narrow that it appears ready to tip over at the touch of a hand. The woods and yards throughout the vicinity display fields of smaller boulders.

SOUTH-WESTERN ONTARIO

Tobermory
59

Georgian Bay

6

Wiarton

Collingwood

Owen Sound
21
49
29
6
34

31
Walkerton
4
24
52

86
55
9
Wroxeter
Orangeville

Goderich
33
Clinton
39
86

Lake Huron
8
45
32
44
38
61
Exeter
Stratford
51
Kitchener-Waterloo
401
21
4
43
Woodstock
42
Blair
46
Lucan
36
30
58
Brantford
Sarnia
Arkona
54
403
402
London
28
56
37
St. Thomas
Port Dover
6
53
48
57
Sparta
54
Chatham
401
Burwell
50
40
60
47
Lake Erie
41
Map not to scale
Windsor
Leamington
Port Stanley
35

London's Blackfriars Bridge is Canada's only arched iron bridge
and the largest to survive in all of North America.

LONDON'S BLACKFRIARS BRIDGE

AMONG ONTARIO'S MANY vanishing heritage features, bridges are the most threatened. Generally, we drive over them and under them but rarely stop to pay attention to them, possibly because they are not easy to see from a moving car. We are just too anxious to get where we are going.

That is one reason why bridges appear in this volume. The five-span stone arch bridge in Pakenham and the last covered bridge at West Montrose are unique in North America. That also describes London's Blackfriars Bridge. Named after its more famous counterpart in London, England, Ontario's Blackfriars Bridge is, at 68.6 metres, the longest single-span iron bowstring bridge in North America, and the only one in Canada.

Iron bridges were the first to begin replacing the wooden bridges that connected pioneer Ontario. While the older wooden structures were quicker and cheaper to build, and often strong, they were prone to rot and fire. Truss bridges made of wrought iron were far stronger and more durable.

Iron bridges owed their popularity to the railway. Because sparks from steam engines would all too often set the wooden bridges ablaze, iron bridges soon began to replace them. Road bridges simply drew upon the designs used by the railway.

In Ontario, the earliest iron road bridges appeared in Brantford, Paris, Peterborough and London. Built in 1875 to cross the north branch of the Thames River, Blackfriars Bridge was the work of Isaac Crouse, a contractor employed by the Wrought Iron Bridge Company of Ohio. The feature that sets this iron bridge apart from others in Ontario is the bowstring, or arched shape. Bowstrings are very rare in iron bridges, and because they were limited in the weight they could carry, iron bowstring bridges were often replaced. But the graceful, curving superstructure gave them an appeal no other iron truss bridge could match.

Frequent improvements over the years have allowed this bridge to continue to carry vehicular traffic, even though other iron bridges in London, such as the King Street bridge, have been decommissioned and converted to pedestrian traffic.

Ontario still claims a bountiful supply of heritage bridges, from the oldest stone bridge in Lyndhurst to the sole surviving suspension bridge on Sewell's Road in Scarborough. Many graceful concrete bowstring bridges still cross the Grand River in many locations, including Caledonia, which boasts one with eight arches. But others, like the awe-inspiring wooden bridge that until 2005 crossed high above the Sioux Narrows, have disappeared. With increasing demands for more and heavier traffic, heritage bridges will continue to succumb to the times.

CASTLES OF THE CUESTA

RUNNING FROM QUEENSTON in the Niagara Peninsula to Tobermory some 400 kilometres to the north, the mighty Niagara Escarpment has been made a UNESCO world biosphere reserve. The escarpment's craggy cliffs are home to an assortment of rare flora and fauna as well as countless waterfalls and stunning views. Many of its water power sites grew into bustling mill towns like Belfountain and Cataract. Its splendid heights attracted wealthy homeowners who built grand castles.

Sitting atop Spirit Rock, overlooking the Georgian Bay port of Wiarton, is the Corran. This grand stone mansion was built by Alexander McNeill in 1881. The seventeen-room castle was decorated with oriental carvings, old weaponry and tapestries. Gardens, lawns and orchards covered its grounds. McNeill named the mansion after his childhood home in Ireland. Corran means "point of land running into the sea."

After McNeill's death the home fell to his son Malcolm, who showed little interest in keeping the property up and sold it in 1960 to a seasonal occupant. Ripe for vandalism, the Corran was set on fire and gutted. Today the haunting stone shell is protected by the local conservation authority.

And if "haunted" is what you are looking for, there is also the sprawling ruin of the Hermitage tucked into the escarpment's Dundas Valley near historic Ancaster. This stone mansion was built in 1830 by the Reverend George Sheed. After changing hands several times, the Hermitage became a hotel in the 1880s. However, fires in 1910 and again in 1934 left the fine buildings a ruined skeleton. Like the Corran, the Hermitage is protected by a conservation authority. The ghost of a jilted lover who hanged himself in the nearby gatehouse is said to haunt the place. The conservation area lies on Mineral Springs Road, west of Hamilton.

A castle that no one protects and that continues to crumble is Osler Castle, high in the Blue Mountains near the town of Collingwood. Built in 1893 by Britton Bath Osler, the castle was intended as a retreat for Osler's wife who, in the smoky city, suffered from asthma. She died shortly after the castle opened to great fanfare, and Osler himself soon followed her. Over the last century, the castle has stood—a lost and forgotten ruin. Its stone walls still stretch above the overgrown meadow around it. The castle can be reached by a side trail running from the Bruce Trail, north of Simcoe County Road 19.

Above: The Corran ruin overlooks the Niagara Escarpment near Wiarton.

Top: The Hermitage, a ruin near Ancaster, is said to be haunted by a jilted lover.

Right: Osler Castle is a lost ruin high in the Blue Mountains near Collingwood.

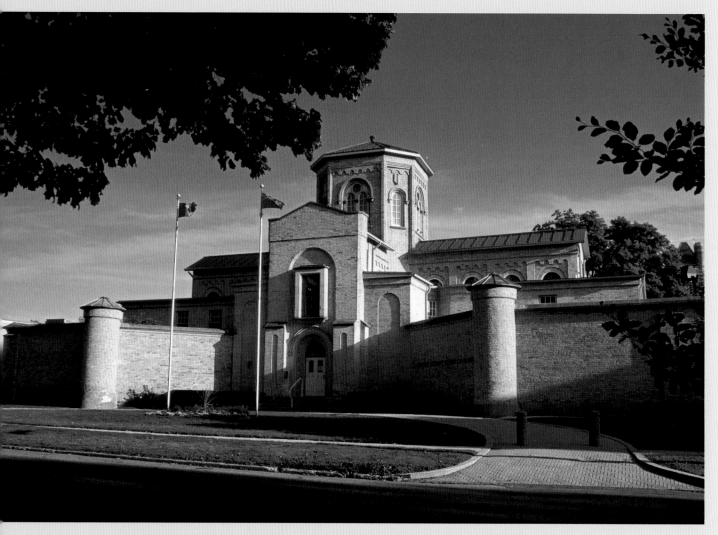

The Oxford County jail in Woodstock is one of Ontario's most stunning architecturally.

Opposite: Thomas Cook was the unfortunate victim of a hangman who made the rope too long. The image of his decapitated head now forms a "death mask" beside the one-time jail's entrance.

WOODSTOCK'S DEATH MASK

PERHAPS IT IS because their stories are sordid or gruesome that Ontario's heritage jails are among the province's least appreciated heritage buildings. From the time Upper Canada governor John Graves Simcoe created Ontario's first four administrative districts, courthouses and their requisite jails began to make their appearance. No town could become a district capital without these buildings.

By 1850, Ontario had evolved into a system of counties. As in the case of Simcoe's districts, each county town — the county's administrative capital — needed to build a courthouse, a registry office and a jail before it could receive the coveted designation. In 1849, the County of Oxford was carved out of the earlier District of London, and Woodstock became its administrative centre. Here a magnificent courthouse was erected and, behind it, an equally stunning jail. Built of yellow brick in an Italianate style, the jail consisted of an octagonal central guard tower from which four long cellblocks radiated.

The first of five felons to be executed in the county jail was Thomas Cook, who in 1862 was convicted for beating his wife to death. It would turn out to be a most bloody hanging.

The duty of an executioner is to ensure that the length of the fateful rope is consistent with the weight of the condemned prisoner. Should the rope be too short for the convict's weight, the unfortunate person would simply dangle until he strangled to death. However, should the rope be too long and the convict too portly, the felon would plung though the trap, gaining speed until, at the end of the rope, the excessive weight would keep the torso going while the head remained tight in the noose. In such cases public spectators were treated to a grisly decapitation. That is the fate that befell the unfortunate Cook.

For reasons that remain unknown — perhaps to prevent a similar occurrence — Cook's likeness has been sculpted into the arch that marks the entrance to the jail. It is Woodstock's death mask.

In 1977, the jail was closed and slated for demolition. However, a spirited fundraising drive by the town's heritage-conscious citizens saved the building, and it now serves as a local health office. And Cook's gaze continues to greet its visitors. The former county jail lies on Buller Street, two blocks north of the main street.

31

Relics of failed farming ring the periphery of the dank Greenock Swamp.

Secrets of the Swamp

THE GREENOCK SWAMP is Ontario's last great wetland. This 8,000-hectare area of impenetrable maples, ferns and muck was once more than seven times its present size and represented the last tract of unsurveyed land in pioneer Ontario.

Although they are now gone, tall, straight white pines grew thick across the swamp, the very species the British navy so zealously sought after. But the swamp would not make life easy for the loggers. During winter — the only time the swamp could be entered — the loggers lived in three camps. To solve the problem of getting the logs out, Henry Cargill, a local lumberman, cut several canals through the dense undergrowth, along which the logs were floated to the mills in the nearby town of Cargill. Following the elder Cargill's death in 1903, his son W. D. took over and built a miniature rail line to haul out the remaining pine.

By the 1920s, the logging was finished, but the Prohibition era was in full swing. What better place to establish illicit moonshine stills than the dark interior of a vast, dense swamp. While those days, too, have long since passed, evidence of the contraband operations continues to be found.

Considered one of the largest wetlands in Ontario, the Greenock Swamp consists of vast tracts of cedar, stands of silver maple, thickets, fens and bogs. The oval-shaped marsh includes ten lakes and a few "islands." Three lobes extend southward from the main body of the swamp. Around the swamp's edges, abandoned fields and sagging log cabins testify to the near impossible conditions early settlers in the area faced. Because of the area's size, biology and scarcity of other wetlands, the Ontario Ministry of Natural Resources has classified it as one of major natural and scientific interest (ANSI).

Despite the logging and whiskey-making activities that once occurred in the swamp, today it is penetrated by a single road. More than half the swamp is owned by the Saugeen Conservation Authority, which is laying out a system of trails. These will allow visitors and scientists to finally get a close look at a stunning example of one of Ontario's vanishing natural heritage landscapes — its great swamps.

The Greenock Swamp lies north of Highway 9, about 20 kilometres west of Walkerton. It is accessed by Concession Road 6 between County Roads 1 and 23.

A TOUCH OF HOLLAND 32

The Bayfield Windmill

A FIELD OF TALL grass bends before the warm summer wind. Above the field, four huge wooden wind sails creak in a slow circle. They belong to North America's only wind-powered saw and grist mill. Located near the Lake Huron port village of Bayfield, it is known as the Folmar Windmill.

Frank de Jong is descended from generations of Dutch millers. Wind-powered sawmills, though rare in Canada, are part of his family heritage and remained in his blood when he migrated to Canada following the Second World War. When he purchased a parcel of land beside the Bayfield River, southeast of Goderich, Ontario, he set about to re-create his own touch of Holland—a saw and grist mill that would be powered by wind alone. Eighteen years went into creating the mill pond on the Bayfield River, and thirteen into building the mill. Its design was based on an actual mill in Holland known as "the Arend." When it was finished, the mill, wind cap and sails towered 29 metres above the Bayfield River marshlands. Although the mill remains privately owned, it is open to the public on a seasonal basis, and indeed has become one of the area's best-known attractions.

For a society accustomed to the ceaseless roar of cars and trucks, the only sounds here are the creaking of the sails. On the main floor of the mill, cables and hooks drag the logs up onto the slipway, where they are pulled slowly forward to the saw blades. These can number from two to twelve. Above the mill, a balcony encircles the wind cap. Above that are the four 22-metre wind sails, which rotate slowly in the wind. The windmill changed hands in 2013, and its future as a tourist attraction became uncertain. It is, however, visible from the road.

The entire area offers plenty to see, from the beautiful and busy tree-lined streets of Bayfield to the strange octagonal main street of Goderich (almost completely rebuilt after the devastating 2011 tornado), and the heritage park in the ghost town of St. Joseph. The Folmar Mill is located south of Huron County Road 13, about 3 kilometres east of Highway 21.

Bayfield's wind-powered sawmill.

CARVED IN STONE
The Apple Park Farm Statues

IF YOU STOP to buy apple cider, apple butter or even plain old apples at the Apple Park Farm, don't be surprised if you get the feeling that you are being watched. Surrounding this attractive brick farmhouse on Highway 8 just east of Goderich are more than fifty stone figures that depict pioneer life in Ontario, or at least one man's view of it.

George Laithwaite moved to the farm from nearby Holmesville in 1895, and for the next sixty years carved from local limestone his depiction of the people and scenes that he saw around him. In pioneer Ontario, with no radio or TV shows to sap the imagination, reading the Bible was a popular pastime. Accordingly, Laithwaite drew from the scriptures scenes for his sculptures of a lion with a lamb and of the Queen of Sheba. He satirized politicians with his portrayal of Sir John A. Macdonald and Sir Robert Borden turning swords into ploughshares. The more raucous aspects of pioneer life appear in the caricatures of a drunken farmhand staggering home supported by his braying donkey, and in four drunken fishermen tottering home from a "fishing" trip.

Early travellers to Goderich soon began to go out of their way to see Laithwaite's sculptures, and at one point they were so popular that he sold postcards from his studio. Although Laithwaite died in 1956, the farm remains in the family. The statues are placed around a 3-acre lawn, while apples, apple cider and apple butter are produced from the 350 trees on the farm.

The farm is on the west side of Highway 8, a short distance southeast of Goderich.

33

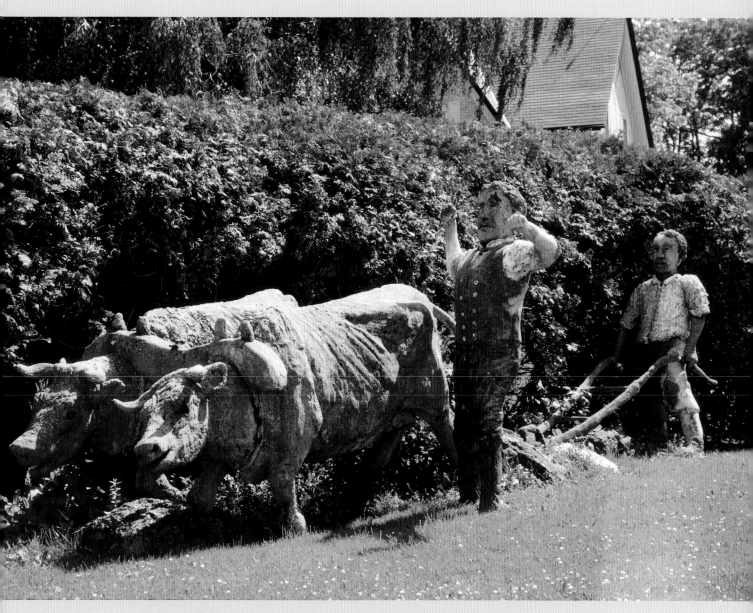

Borden and Macdonald have turned their "swords" into ploughshares.

Opposite: One of the more rollicking of the Park Farm statues.

THE HOLE IN THE HILL
The Strange Story of the Eugenia Arches

DRY MOST OF the year, and unknown to most Ontario travellers, Eugenia Falls in the Beaver Valley has been the site of some strange activities. In the 1850s, a case of mistaken identity led to a short-lived gold rush. Mistaking the shiny lustre of iron pyrite for gold, a pair of hunters sparked a flurry of digging and panning until the shine proved to be only fool's gold.

The next venture was more practical. In the 1870s, William Hogg from Hogg's Hollow, just north of Toronto, bought land adjacent to the falls and built a small electric plant to provide power to a few local communities. Buoyed by his success, Hogg went back to Toronto to try to sell city officials his power for their expanding streetcar system; however, the Adam Beck plant at Niagara Falls was closer and more reliable, so Toronto's politicians sent a dejected Hogg back to Eugenia.

In 1903 a group of Toronto businessmen formed the Georgian Bay Power Company and tried once again to capitalize on the questionable power potential of the falls. To maximize the drop, they excavated a tunnel through the hill beside the falls to the bottom of the valley far below. They began digging the tunnel in 1906, but unexpected problems with quicksand pushed the cost to over $1 million. Still, by 1907 the tunnel was finished. At 264 metres long, 2.7 metres high and 2.6 metres wide, it was big enough to drive a buggy through. And someone did just that.

Perhaps it was pride of workmanship, but the distinguishing features of the tunnel were the beautiful stone arches at either end, described by some as Roman in appearance. The plant never did operate, and the tunnel remained dry. Instead, a dam was built at Eugenia Lake itself, from which an even greater and more reliable fall of water could supply a larger plant built further down the Beaver Valley. For many years the wooden flumes remained a landmark in the Beaver Valley, but they have since been removed.

Although the tunnels themselves have long collapsed, the arches have withstood weathering and erosion. They are located in the Eugenia Falls Conservation Area, in the village of Eugenia, which lies on Grey County Road 13. The larger and more complete of the two arches stands near the brink of the falls on the opposite side of the river from the path and parking lot. (For safety reasons, the park authority discourages visitors from crossing the river above the falls.) The second arch, near the base of the hill, has collapsed and can be found only after a long and steep hike and a bit of luck.

34

The entrance to the long-lost tunnel at Eugenia.

POINT PELEE

Where Canada Begins

35

S TAND HERE AND all of Canada is north of you. So, for that matter, is northern California. At 42 degrees north latitude, Point Pelee is the most southerly part of mainland Canada and lies south of much of the continental United States. Such a southern latitude also provides the point with a range of southern vegetation found nowhere else in Ontario, vegetation more common, in fact, to the Carolinas. Even prickly pear cactus is found here. Indeed, the rare plant and animal life earned the point its status as one of Canada's first national parks.

But its history goes back far beyond that. Owing to Point Pelee's strategic location,

well into Lake Erie and close to American shipping lanes, the British military in the 1790s set the point aside as a naval reserve. That didn't stop a handful of squatters, known as "Pointers," from moving in and starting up fishing and small-time farming.

The sandy soil limited the range of crops, and the point gradually became more popular with hunters and birdwatchers. Then, in 1918, through the efforts of ornithologist Percy Taverner and his bird-lover friend Jack Miner (founder of the nearby Jack Miner Bird Sanctuary), the government of Canada designated the reserve as a national park.

Commercial fishing operations persisted

Point Pelee is Canada's most southerly point of land.

until the last lease expired in 1969, and a few cottagers hung around even after that. Nature lovers now arrive from around the world to enjoy the rare plants and animals, but especially the spectacular fall migration of the beautiful monarch butterfly, during which branches of trees are entirely enveloped in the orange-and-black creatures.

Park planners have made the park's many features easy to see. Boardwalks guide nature lovers through the vast marshes, and pathways lead them to the cactus patch. Even one of the old squatter shacks has been preserved for history buffs.

But the most unusual experience in the park is the point itself. After the trees end, a bare sand spit leads another 1.25 kilometres into the lake. (This, some believe, gave the point its name, the word Pelee meaning "bald," or "peeled," in French.) The point narrows until it becomes a pencil point and then fades into waves. But you can walk beyond even that into the shallow waters of Lake Erie and look back on Canada — all of it.

The remarkable landform lies at the end of County Road 33, south of Leamington.

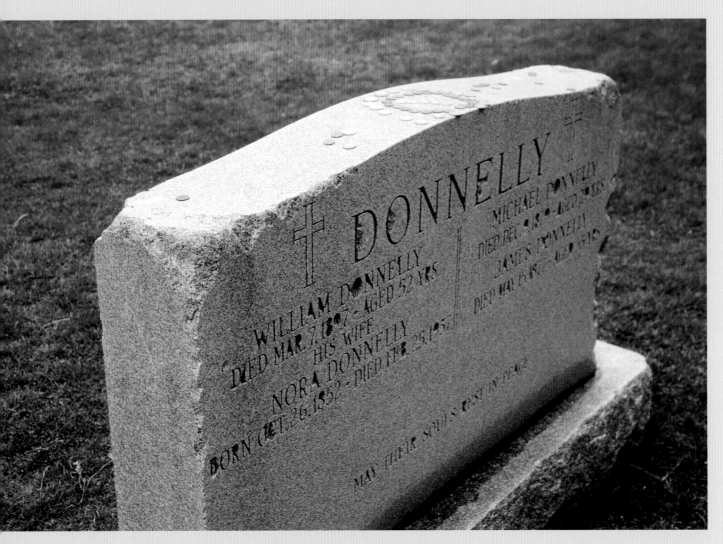

36

The Donnelly tombstone still sees many visitors.

THE TELLTALE GRAVE
The Donnelly Tombstone

IT'S OKAY TO go to Lucan these days and talk about the Donnellys. But a century ago all of North America was talking about the "Black Donnellys" and their untimely demise.

On a bitterly cold night in February 1880, a local vigilante gang attacked two homes belonging to a family of Irish immigrants named the Donnellys, and brutally butchered five of their number. Members of several prominent local families stood accused of the gristly slaughter, among them the sheriff.

Daily newspaper reports of the trial kept the English-speaking world transfixed for months. The first trial resulted in a hung jury. In the second, the judge, allegedly following instructions from his political masters who were seeking re-election, ordered the jury to disregard the testimony of a youthful witness, and the vigilantes went free.

The massacre was the result of an ancient Irish feud and a bitter business rivalry, all played out in an era when drunkenness and violence were part of pioneer life. Eventually the feud reached such a fever pitch that beatings and burnings became routine, and many of them were blamed on the large Donnelly clan.

Lucan is one of those down-to-earth towns where many residents can still trace their roots back to the first pioneers. Several had grandparents or great-grandparents who were part of the simmering feud, and even a few who were part of the mob. Time has eased, if not altogether erased, the bitterness. The Lucan Area Heritage and Donnelly Museum at 171 Main Street in Lucan recounts the tragedy, while the current owner of the homestead property hosts group tours (by appointment only), vividly re-enacting the events of that deadly night. The house on the site now was built by one of the surviving sons after the original cabin crashed in flames the night of the murders, marked only by stones laid at the cabin's four corners.

The "Swamp Schoolhouse" where the vigilantes hatched their plot still stands, used now as storage shed. But the strongest reminder of that night lies in the graveyard of St. Patrick's Roman Catholic church, the very church where the sworn enemies had even worshipped together. That reminder is the marble headstone listing all the names of the family members who were cut down that night.

The original marker, now secreted away in a northern Ontario basement, used the word "murdered" to describe their demise, but vandalism forced its removal. Today's stone says simply "died." The graveyard lies at the corner of Highway 4 and the Roman Line, about 25 kilometres north of London, Ontario. The homestead itself is about 6 kilometres north of that.

ONTARIO'S BLACK GOLD
The Petrolia Discovery

So VAST, MODERN and international has today's petroleum industry become that its modest roots have been forgotten. And those roots go back to a little town in south-western Ontario aptly named Petrolia, where today a non-profit foundation, Petrolia Discovery, is striving to keep the legacy alive.

And it is succeeding. On the east end of Petrolia, the foundation operates a most unusual park. Here, on one of Canada's original oil fields, you can find oil rigs that date back a century. A central pumping plant known as a Fitzgerald Rig contains the biggest drive wheel ever built for a jerker rod system and has been operating off and on since 1903. From this building, wooden jerker rods slide back and forth across the oil field to operate pumps that urge oil from the ground. You can also see the gum beds that drew the first oil explorers to the area, and a cribbed well that shows how, at first, oil was dug rather than drilled.

Although Oil Springs, 12 kilometres south, represents the site of North America's first commercial oil well, dating from 1858, Petrolia contained the larger deposits. By 1866 the town had become a boom town of three thousand and a branch-line terminus for both the Grand Trunk Railway and the Canada Southern Railway.

Then, with the formation of the Imperial Oil Company in 1880, Petrolia became the centre of the British Empire's oil industry, a title it would retain for nearly twenty years. In that period, drillers and riggers travelled to all corners of the world, including countries like Iran and Iraq, to share the knowledge and skills that had quickly become legendary.

After the First World War, new refineries at Sarnia, along with the discovery of vast new reserves in Alberta, turned Petrolia into a near ghost town. But Petrolia Discovery has turned all that around. By bringing to the present a living snapshot of the oil industry's past, the park has revived the town. Local businesses have pumped money into streetscaping, while a costly restoration of the grand Victoria Hall has restored summer theatre to the town. A walking tour takes in the grand mansions of the oil barons, while a 4-kilometre fitness trail follows the ruins of the original oil fields.

At the site of the first well, the Oil Springs museum recounts that chapter in Ontario's oil history, although sadly, the village of Oil Springs has retained few oil heritage buildings. However, a short country drive takes you past privately owned fields where jerker rods still pull the crude from the ground as they have for a century and a half.

Petrolia is on County Road 4, about 30 kilometres southeast of Sarnia.

37

The Petrolia Discovery theme park near the site of North America's first commercial well contains rigs and derricks that date back to the 19th century.

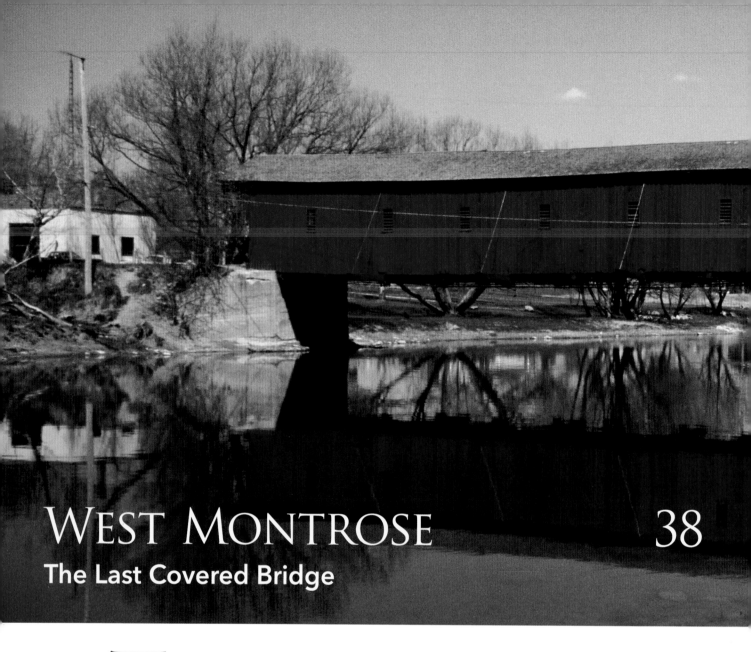

WEST MONTROSE
The Last Covered Bridge

38

THE CLATTER OF hoofbeats and the groaning of a wagon wheel echo among the wooden rafters of the old covered bridge. A scene for a western movie? No, an everyday event at West Montrose, 15 kilometres north of Waterloo, just off Regional Road 22.

The area is heavily populated by the Old Order, "horse-and-buggy" Mennonites, and these black-garbed traditionalists frequently guide their horse-drawn wagons or buggies through what is Ontario's last covered bridge.

In an era when wood was less expensive and commonly used for bridge construction, walls and roofs were often added to

prevent the deterioration caused by rain and heavy snow. Despite the utility and popularity of this style in eastern Canada, Ontario's British army road builders steered clear of it, and fewer than a dozen such bridges were built in this province. The one at West Montrose is the only survivor.

Built in 1881 by a Mennonite barn builder named John Baer, it remained the Grand River's only crossing in the area until 1960, when a new concrete structure was completed less than a kilometre away. The bridge measures 60 metres long, and was illuminated by twenty shuttered windows and coal-oil lanterns, later replaced by electric lights. A feature rarely found on other

Of Ontario's historic covered bridges, the one at West Montrose on the Grand River is the only survivor.

covered bridges is the 1.8-metre overhang above each entrance.

To allow continued use of the historic structure, truss reinforcements have been added to the inside, the roof has been re-shingled and the substructure replaced. To complement this postcard scene, the village of West Montrose, huddled around the western approach to the bridge, has retained many of its simple nineteenth-century buildings. A part of pioneer Ontario can be both seen and heard at the West Montrose covered bridge.

The Grand River boasts many heritage bridges along its 300-kilometre course. In fact, the river contains Ontario's greatest concentration of historic bowstring bridges, with graceful arches above the road. The longest is the eight-arch bridge in Caledonia, while six-arch structures span the river in Freeport and Bridgeport.

SLOMAN'S SCHOOL CAR
The Schoolhouse that Rode the Rails

FOR DECADES SCHOOLHOUSES dotted the Ontario countryside. Few of us, however, are aware that, through the wilds of northern Ontario, where only the railways linked little settlements isolated by miles of bush, the schoolhouses were in railway cars.

Between 1880 and 1914, five railway lines made their way through the forests of New Ontario, as the north was then called. At railside there grew a string of mill towns and hamlets for railway maintenance workers. But only a handful of towns grew large enough to support their own schools.

By 1922, the population of these outposts was substantial, yet they had few facilities, no luxuries and no schools. A North Bay school superintendent named J. B. McDougall pleaded with the then Ontario premier, G. Howard Ferguson, to initiate a six-month experiment that would bring to the settlements a school on the back of a train.

Passenger cars were altered into classrooms containing desks, books, blackboards and a small apartment for the teacher. In 1926 the first two cars departed their display areas at the Canadian National Exhibition for northeastern Ontario. The experiment proved so successful that it was quickly made into a permanent program, and by 1938 seven such cars were operating across the northland.

For four days at a time the cars would rest at a siding in the tiny settlements, while children hiked or sledded for several kilometres for their precious education. Night school was provided for adults, and the schoolcars became social gathering places for the area.

However, during the 1950s, the trackside settlements faded. The advent of diesel and a massive highway-building program turned them into ghost towns, and the schoolcars were no longer needed. One of the last, CNR No. 15089, was shunted unceremoniously into a Toronto railyard in 1967.

After spending a few years with the Ontario Rail Association, car 15089 was put up for sale. A former student noticed the ad and eagerly phoned the family of the car's last teacher, Fred Sloman.

To their credit, the people of Clinton, the home of Fred Sloman's widow, Cela, rallied behind the cause and brought the car to Clinton, where it was restored to its appearance as a schoolcar and opened as a museum. While many a country schoolhouse has received new life as a residence, the schoolhouse that rode on rails is one of a kind, and retells a story of northern life that would otherwise be forgotten.

To reach the museum, follow Highway 4 south from Highway 8 within the town of Clinton.

39

The School on Wheels, Clinton, Ontario.

40

Once pallisaded, these prehistoric earthworks now appear as grassy mounds.

THE SOUTHWOLD EARTHWORKS
A Pre-European-Contact Village Site

THE FLATLANDS OF Elgin County stretch along the shores of Lake Erie, yielding some of Ontario's most fertile farmlands. Where the few forests remain, they contain Carolinian flora species. And farming has removed nearly all traces of early habitations. All except the unusual Southwold Earthworks.

Now a National Historic Site, these barely discernible lumps of earth represent a village site occupied by the Attiwonderonk prior to European contact, a Native group whose territory stretched from Chatham to Niagara Falls. Built about the time that Christopher Columbus was wandering around the Caribbean, the site consists of two circular mounds of earth separated by an apparent moat structure. The mounds represent the double row of palisades that surrounded the village, with gaps to indicate where a stream meandered through the site.

Research concludes that the outer mound is the older of the two. The palisades were built of tree trunks 4 to 5 metres high, driven into the ground and embanked with earth. The inner, or later, palisade consisted of two rows of trunks, indicating perhaps a concern for greater security. The double palisade is the site's most archaeologically significant component. Inside the compound were a number of the traditional longhouses, while fields of maize and squash surrounded the village.

By the time the first Europeans began ploughing the ground, likely during the Thomas Talbot settlements of the 1820s, the tribe had long vanished, possibly having fled the deadly Iroquois incursions of the 1640s. What is most astonishing about the site is that it survived the pioneer period, when homesteaders would not likely have recognized the site for what it was, nor cared. One wonders how many similar heritage treasures were lost to the plough during that time.

Despite its national heritage status, the site is barely developed. The only parking is along a widened shoulder on the road. Informational plaques indicate how the site was arranged, while a grassy pathway leads the quarter kilometre from the road into the stand of trees where the earthworks can be seen. The Southwold Earthworks are situated just south of Iona on County Road 14, about 3 kilometres south of Highway 3.

OJIBWAY

The Case of the Missing Town

41

ACROSS ONTARIO, TOWNS were mapped out. Some remained small, some boomed, and some never made it off paper. But rarely were the sidewalks, hydrants and roads built only to remain empty and unused.

Windsor, Ontario, grew in a most unusual way. While most towns started small, perhaps around a mill site or a port, Windsor was an amalgamation of planned company towns. The first settlement was known as Sandwich, and grew around a trading post on the Detroit River, later becoming the county seat.

Walkerville was laid out around Hiram Walker's whiskey distillery. Its neighbour, Ford City, was incorporated in 1913 as a residential community for the Ford company's automotive plant.

Then there was Ojibway.

Ojibway differed from Walkerville and Ford City. While these predecessors used a traditional grid network of streets, Ojibway represented the latest in town planning. Streets radiated outward from three central squares, while a four-lane expressway linked it with Windsor, then 7 kilometres away.

Ojibway was to be an 1,800-acre company town for the American-Canadian Steel Corporation. Construction started during the First World War and continued into the 1920s. Objections, however, from Canadian steel producers, the effects of the Depression, and the presence of massive underground salt deposits beneath the proposed streets halted the project.

Although a few industrial buildings were completed, and the roads and sidewalks built, the population remained below one hundred. Over the rest of the townsite, grass and weeds claimed the streets and sidewalks, while forests took hold of the undeveloped area. By the 1960s, Ojibway had earned the distinction of being Canada's smallest organized municipality, with a population of a mere six.

Following Ojibway's inevitable annexation to Windsor in 1966, suburban growth spread onto the old townsite. New housing appeared on some of the original streets, and a racetrack was built in the middle of the "town." But much remained undeveloped. Grandly named streets like Broadview and Ojibway Parkway curved past open fields, where rusting hydrants poked above the tall grasses, while part of the planned four-lane express route became a

This concrete sidewalk, once slated to serve homes, leads only through a silent woodlot.

local lane named Sandwich Street. But the strangest sights of all in this strangest of towns are the concrete sidewalks that cut straight through mature woodlots.

To reach the forest with the sidewalks, follow Normandy Street east from Malden. The doglegs in the first road following Ellis Street and Washington Boulevard represent the proposed streets, which now lead only through the woods. Concrete sidewalks line these dirt lanes, and at regular intervals cut straight into the forests.

Many of Ontario's communities have a strange history, but there are none so strange as Ojibway, the missing town.

LAST OF A KIND

Blair's Sheave Tower

42

THE WOODEN TOWER stands in the middle of the woods near the historic community of Blair, looking like a miniature mining headframe. But this tapering wooden structure, which rises four storeys above a rushing stream, is a rare relic of pioneer Ontario — a sheave tower.

Sheave towers were accessories to grist mills. They used the force of the river to turn a sheave, or grooved wheel, and were connected by a pulley to a water-powered grist mill. A local mill owner named Allan Bowman built the tower at Blair in 1876 to power the nearby Carlisle grist mill. The original mill, a five-storey structure built in 1849, burned in 1928. Following the fire, the power from the sheave tower produced electricity until 1954.

Long a favourite of local artists, photographers and historians, it was partially restored in 1962 by the Waterloo Historical Society. Runoff from nearby housing developments, however, rushed into the creek, where it damaged the foundation and put the building's future at risk.

Blair, however, is one of those heritage-conscious communities. So while the owners of the tower worked to clear the sluiceway of silt, the local council voted, in 1986, to declare it a heritage structure, to help reduce the threat of demolition. In 1994 it was bought, in turn, by the Cambridge chapter of the Architectural Conservancy of Ontario.

Four years later renowned heritage architect Nicholas Hill was hired to restore the crumbling ruin. Hill had been responsible for more than a dozen community heritage plans, as well as restoration of the Kingsville, Ontario, railway station and the University of Guelph's Cruickston Park mansion and grounds.

Because much of the tower's wood had rotted, many original planks required replacing. But in 2000, the restored tower was unveiled to commemorate the village's two hundredth anniversary.

The heritage of Blair goes beyond the sheave tower. The village began life as a milling centre on Blair Creek, close to the Grand River, where today, the urban sprawl from Cambridge creeps ever closer. Yet the historic integrity of Blair continues to survive, as hotels, homes, mills and cemeteries that date from the early days of settlement have been retained. But of all the saved and restored historic buildings, the sheave tower, the only one of its kind left in Ontario, remains the most unusual.

The tower lies in the woods on Mill Lane, west of Blair Road.

Blair's strange sheave tower resembles a miniture mining headframe.

KITCHENER'S PIONEER TOWER

43

Cultural Cooperation

THE KITCHENER AREA is Ontario's capital of unusual towers. Besides the rustic sheave tower near Blair, Kitchener has the stone pioneer tower.

Dominating the Grand River Valley from one of its loftiest banks, the tower was built to commemorate Ontario's first inland pioneers. French settlements had existed along the Detroit River and United Empire Loyalists had settled along the shores of Lake Ontario and Lake Erie. Joseph Schoerg and Samuel Betzner arrived in 1800 and were the vanguard of Ontario's inland pioneers.

By 1805, the German Company had purchased over 60,000 acres of land along the Grand River from the Mohawks, who had received it as a reward for their service to the British during the American Revolution. Soon, columns of Conestoga wagons were lumbering northward carrying Pennsylvania Dutch and Mennonite settlers. These savvy farmers, with their commitment to farming as a divinely ordained way of life, established one of Ontario's most prolific agricultural communities.

The idea for the tower came more than a century later. To help heal the nationalist wounds caused by the First World War, and to celebrate the German origins of the Waterloo area, William Breithaupt promoted the idea of a pioneer memorial tower.

Designed by Toronto architect W. A. Langton, the tower was officially opened August 28, 1926, and was immediately declared a National Historic Site. The 22-metre-high tower is topped with a copper spire of Swiss influence and a weather vane that commemorates the arrival of the colonists in their Conestoga wagons. The body of the tower is faced with fieldstones to reflect the hardships in clearing the fields. Visitors enter through a doorway of Indiana limestone and climb to an eight-sided observation deck. In 1939, concerned over declining maintenance, the Historic Sites Branch took over the tower and upgraded the grounds, planting grass and adding a parking area.

Farm buildings of the pioneering Betzner and Schoerg families still stand nearby. In the 0.5-hectare park beside the tower, their family graves are the oldest non-Aboriginal inland burial grounds in Ontario. The tower is not staffed and has no admission charge. It lies at the end of Pioneer Tower Road, which you can reach by following Deer Ridge Drive east from Kitchener's King Street. The site is part of the Woodside National Historic Site in Kitchener.

This stone tower commemorates the heritage of the German pioneers in the Waterloo region.

THE CRYPTIC GRAVESTONE

44

Rushes Cemetery

VISITORS TO THE Rushes pioneer cemetery, west of Kitchener, have long scratched their heads in puzzlement at the mass of letters that cover the strange grave marker. While the size of the stone and the graphic etched on it are not unlike those found on thousands of other nineteenth-century grave markers, the message definitely is not. For covering the entire face of the gravestone is a mass of 225 letters and numbers with no apparent order or sense. Yet the message is in there, if you can figure it out.

Rushes Cemetery is an ordinary-looking pioneer cemetery. Situated atop a hill, the cemetery is neatly trimmed and surrounded by rolling farmland. Cars rush past on the busy road, while an occasional Mennonite buggy creaks by at a more leisurely pace. But it is in the far corner of Rushes cemetery that the now famous "Bean marker," with its cryptic inscription, attracts the most attention.

Samuel Bean was born in 1842 in Wilmot Township, and became an Evangelist minister as well as a medical doctor. Local legend claims he also read the entire Bible sixty-five times. In 1865 he married Henrietta Furry, who died only seven months later. His second marriage, to Susanna Clegg, didn't last much longer. To commemorate their passing, Bean devised what may be one of Ontario's most mystifying and most-visited grave markers, with what at first glance is a nonsensical and random arrangement of letters that totally cover the front of the marker.

While the dedication may appear impossible to decipher, by determining where to start the message and the order in which the words are spelled, the message is suddenly and plainly revealed. The original grave marker had deteriorated to the point where the letters became unreadable. But to help keep alive this interesting piece of local lore, heritage proponents in 1982 erected a duplicate stone beside the original.

Happily, Bean's third marriage lasted longer and he now lies buried by his third wife in the cemetery in Strasbourg, Ontario.

The grave marker itself is illustrated here, and the reader is invited to try and solve the puzzle. Clue: don't start at either the top or the bottom. Rather, begin at the seventh column from the left, and at the seventh letter from the top. The answer is at the back of this book.

Rushes cemetery is located 3 kilometres north of the attractive country village of Wellesley, on Waterloo Regional Road 5.

Can you solve the message on this odd grave marker? *See page 271 for the answer.*

THE SUDDEN SPLENDOUR 45 OF THE ELORA GORGE

SUDDENLY AND UNEXPECTEDLY, in the flat farmlands northwest of Guelph, there appears a crack. No ordinary crack, the Elora Gorge is a canyon 2 kilometres long and more than 20 metres deep — a wonderland of hanging gardens, caves, caverns, dry valleys and odd-looking rock formations.

The gorge represents the outcropping of a dolostone formation known by geologists as the Guelph Formation, rich in fossils and reefs, and four hundred million years old. When the glaciers left the area about twenty thousand years ago, the waters began to wear down the rock until a long gorge took shape. The remnant of that post-glacial torrent is today's Grand River.

The various shapes and formations found in the gorge have fanciful names. Dividing the river into a foaming waterfall, the Tooth of Time is formed by the remains of an eroded ledge. Close by, the Lovers' Leap promontory juts into the fork formed by Irwin Creek and the Grand River. Farther downstream, the waters of a long-vanished river that plunged over the edge of the cliff carved a series of rock columns that resemble castle ramparts. An extinct waterfall has carved out a 40-metre-wide amphitheatre known as the Punch Bowl.

The Cascade is the filmy plunge of a small creek into the gully. Across from it the Hanging Garden shows off various mosses and ferns drooping from an overhanging cliff. Several caves along the riverbank make unusual swimming holes, and the Hole in the Wall provides passage for a trail right through the rock itself.

But hidden under the nearby farmlands there also lies an earlier, pre-glacial gorge, which parallels today's defile. While the existence of this mystery gorge is revealed only through the drilling of local wells, it can be seen near Fergus where the route of the earlier gorge crosses that of the newer one, causing the rocky wall of today's gorge to vanish at that point.

The strange beauty and the appeal of the rushing river have turned the gorge into a popular park. Trails follow both riverbanks and wind along the bottom of the gorge. Inner tubes are rented to those who wish to cool off on a hot summer day by floating downstream and viewing the gorge in its entirety and without obstruction.

The Elora Gorge Conservation Area, which also has campgrounds, is a short distance southwest of the popular village of Elora.

This unexpected crack in flat farmland contains many unusual rock formations.

Fossil hunters can dig the ancient critters right out of the mud.

FOSSIL HUNTERS' FANTASY
The Rock Glen Gorge

WHILE NO ONE is going to find any dinosaur bones in the Rock Glen Gorge, they will find hundreds of equally ancient creatures. Located in the Rock Glen Conservation Area, the gorge was created by the relentless erosion of the Ausable River into layers of limestone and shale. As the ancestors of today's shellfish died they drifted to the bottom of an early ocean, where they hardened into rock. Above them, more layers were deposited, and they also hardened. When the last glaciers finally melted, the water of today's Ausable River eroded into the soil and then into bedrock to gradually expose the former seabeds and their trove of early critters.

Fossils appear in much of Ontario's bedrock, and most usually require a pick to remove. But what makes the fossils in the damp little gully so unusual is that, during rainfalls, the shale turns soft enough to allow the shells to be removed by hand. The most common fossils found here are the branch-like staghorn coral or plant-like crinoids. Less common are the snail-like trilobites. The most interesting are the butterfly-shaped brachiopods, which the Chinese call "stone butterflies." While the fossils can be found throughout the little valley, the footing is tricky. The hunting grounds lie deep in the 25-metre chasm,

where the stream trickles around boulders.

Rock Glen Conservation Authority has a few rules. Picks and shovels are not permitted, nor is collecting from the valley walls themselves. Loose sediments, however, are everywhere, and here you can help yourself. The park has a museum and staff with helpful brochures. The 25-hectare conservation area is on Lambton County Road 12, close to the village of Arkona, in south-western Ontario.

THE BIG SAND PILE 47
Houghton's Sand Hill

TOWERING MORE THAN 120 metres above the waters of Lake Erie, Ontario's biggest sandbox, the Houghton Sand Hill, stands higher than even the Scarborough Bluffs. As the glaciers of the last great ice age melted northward, a huge lake, four times the size of Lake Erie, formed along the edge of the ice lobe. As the torrents of meltwater raced into the lake, a huge delta took shape. The glaciers melted back still farther, allowing the great lake to drain away, leaving today's Lake Erie and a monster pile of sand. The winds began to blow across the treeless wasteland, and the sand piled into huge dunes that towered above the lake.

Thousands of years later, as settlers took up land in the nearby forests, this geological phenomenon did not go unnoticed. In 1877, the *Atlas of Norfolk County*, normally a conservative and understated tome, gushed uncharacteristically that there was "nothing more astonishing than the immense mounds of pure sand, standing upon the edge of the precipitous cliffs which border the lake."

One of the first to take advantage of the heights was the United States Lake Survey, which placed an 18-metre observatory on the summit. A similar tower on Long Point, and a third across the lake in Pennsylvania, helped map the navigation charts used by sailors to this day.

The sand hill attracted curiosity seekers as well. In the 1890s, George Alton, the owner, charged ten cents a visit. A geological oddity was quickly becoming a tourist attraction. But the hill came perilously close to extinction when a glass manufacturer tried to purchase the sand for export to the United States. Alton resisted, and the sand pile was saved.

Then in 1958 a campground was opened. Constant improvements to the unusual grounds have made it one of the more popular privately owned attractions on Lake Erie. From the roadside, the hill looks like an uninspiring grassy mound. A short walk to the top reveals the dizzying height above the lake below. Pure sand from crest to beach, the bluffs display ever-changing layers and shapes.

Sand Hill Park is located 12 kilometres east of Port Burwell on Regional Road 42.

Ontario's biggest "sandbox" towers 120 metres above Lake Erie.

48

Ontario's only adobe blacksmith shop is preserved as a museum in Sparta.

A Bit of "Old Mexico"
Sparta's Adobe Blacksmith Shop

SPARTA'S MAIN STREET offers one of the most eclectic arrays of main street buildings in the province.

Take, for example, the former tinsmith shop. Built around 1840, it displays the unusual board-and-batten method of siding and boasts the false facade of a "boom town" storefront. Beside it stands a house built in the Quaker style of construction by the village smithy, John Ollie.

Clustered around the main intersection are two former hotels — the Sparta House on the southwest corner, which functioned as a temperance hall, and the Sparta Hotel on the northwest corner. The Sparta Hotel stands two and a half storeys high with a full-length wooden porch.

The old general store occupies the southeast corner, looking much like many of Ontario's traditional stores.

Sparta dates from the exodus of American Quakers, a pacifist sect, who refused to serve in the American army during the War of 1812. In 1813, Quaker Jonathon Doan acquired some 1,200 hectares on a millstream. Naming the place after the village he was forced to flee south of the border, Doan laid out a townsite. Through the 1830s and '40s, it boomed to include mills, stores and churches. But after 1875, when the railways reached St. Thomas several miles to the north, Sparta's growth stagnated.

As a result, many of the structures from Sparta's boom times have survived — among them, a blacksmith shop built unlike any other in Ontario. Like homes and stores more commonly found in older neighbourhoods in Mexico, the shop was built of adobe brick — a mixture of clay and straw all trampled in a pit by a team of horses. Constructed in 1827, the shop has walls two feet thick, which remain exposed to view.

That is not to say no other building in Ontario was made in the adobe style. But those that were are now covered with siding or stucco. Sparta's adobe blacksmith shop is the only one whose "Old Mexico" style of construction has not been concealed — on the outside or within.

Having ceased operation as a blacksmith shop in 1944, the building now houses Ye Olde Forge and Anvil Museum, operated by the Sparta and District Historical Society. Another house opposite was also constructed of abode brick, but those bricks are now covered over by siding.

Today the blacksmith shop and the other village stores have become a popular day-trip destination for residents of nearby cities like London, Kitchener and Hamilton. Also close at hand is the Lake Erie village of Port Stanley, with its fleet of fishing boats and popular Port Stanley Terminal Rail tour train. Sparta lies along County Road 27, about 25 kilometres southeast of St. Thomas.

ONTARIO'S WORST ROADS

49

The Forgotten Corduroy Trails

No matter how much we deride our deteriorating roads, with their washboards and potholes, no road was more painful to travel than the corduroy roads of pioneer Ontario. To allow horses and wagons to cross low-lying areas, which were bogs during the spring season, logs were laid side by side. The effect resembled the ridged cloth preferred by European royalty, and they were named "corduroy" or "cords-du-roi" roads.

The first roads in Ontario simply followed the trails tramped by the Aboriginal inhabitants. These followed the higher grounds between main waterways and avoided obstacles. Then, as the surveyors marched through the forests, clearing the first military roads, they cared little for anything that got in the way, and laid the roads with straight military precision. Swamps were simply dealt with by the use of the hated log roads.

Early pioneer diaries lamented the tossing and the lurching that tormented their authors as they bounced over the irregular and rotting sections of corduroy. Eventually, as more settlers arrived, the roads were graded and gravelled, and finally, with the advent of the auto age, paved.

Not too surprisingly, the original log trails are nearly impossible to find anymore. Not only has rot and resurfacing obliterated them, but they have been almost totally ignored by heritage preservationists, which makes the few places where they can still be seen unusual.

One of the clearest and longest stretches of such road lies on a hiking trail in Awenda Provincial Park, north of Midland. It was once used as a logging road through this forested recreation area. In Killarney Provincial Park, the Silhouette Trail includes corduroy logging roads as well, as does the trail in Rawhide Conservation Area, 35 kilometres north of Elliot Lake. Parts of Muskoka Road 14 between Fraserburg and Pine Lake have been neglected to the point that the old logs are making their way to the surface, to the dismay of local residents. Also in Muskoka, the Buckwallow Trail follows corduroy sections of the original Peterson Colonization Road. And in the Beaver Valley, east of Kimberley, another old section of corduroy road forms part of a local trail.

Likely there remain other long-forgotten segments of log road that lurk yet on abandoned portions of Ontario's earliest roads.

A section of original corduroy road survives in a swampy section of the Beaver Valley.

50

The flag station at Union, still in use, is North America's smallest "Union Station."

The Smallest Union Station

WHAT IS THE size of a two-hole outhouse and attracts tourists from across the continent? The answer is North America's smallest "Union Station." In railway terminology, a union station is one shared by more than one railway company, and more often than not they are large, urban terminals. Therefore, when train travellers think of Union Station, they picture the high-vaulted concourse of Toronto's Union Station, or the grand facade of that in Washington, D.C. They are not likely to envisage the tiny grey-flag station that guards the track of the Port Stanley Terminal Railway. The station's name derives not from its size or its function, but simply from the name of a nearby hamlet, Union.

Not only is it the oldest building on the once-busy line, but the style and the arched windows reveal that railway architects often paid as much attention to the tiny flag stations as they did to the larger and more elegant city stations.

Today's Port Stanley Terminal Railway was resurrected as a labour of love from the near ruins of the pioneering London and Port Stanley Railway. Originally built to carry lumber and farm products from the southwestern farmlands to the wharves at Port Stanley, and to link with the Grand Trunk Railway in London, it eventually became a busy excursion line. Londoners crowded into the coaches at that city's now long-demolished brick-and-stone station to go to the Lake Erie beaches, or to dance to the big bands that played the internationally renowned Stork Club.

Eventually CN took over the line and, after a few years of dwindling traffic, closed it. While other stations were demolished, the little flag station at Union was given little thought. When the line was abandoned, Union Station, deteriorating and overgrown, miraculously still stood.

Local rail enthusiasts purchased the line and, after pouring countless hours and money from their own pockets into its repair, have restored passenger rides from Port Stanley to a new replica station in downtown St. Thomas. Awaiting the passengers halfway along is the smallest Union Station, restored, repainted, and housing old photos and railway memorabilia.

You can board the excursion trains at the larger station in Port Stanley and travel the few miles up the line to Union and St. Thomas, or, if the trains aren't running that day, you can follow the Golf Club Road west to the little station from Highway 4 in Union.

3-D-CEPTION
The Trompe l'Oeil Murals of Castle Kilbride

LIKE MOST NINETEENTH-CENTURY mansions, Castle Kilbride is a monument to the excesses of the Industrial Age. Born to a Scottish weaver, James Livingston arrived in Canada in 1854 at the age of sixteen, where he worked first on a farm, then in a flax mill. In 1864, along with his brother, he rented a flax mill in the village of Wellesley. Within just three years the pair had built their own flax mill in Baden, adding a linseed-oil mill to their operation. Linseed oil was a key ingredient in paint and soap, and in high demand in Ontario's booming cities.

In 1877, Livingston, known as the "Flax and Oil King of Canada," decided to build his "castle." Set back from the road, surrounded by a wrought-iron fence and topped with an Italianate belvedere, Castle Kilbride quickly became a local landmark.

The elegance was evident on the exterior, but it was the inside that drew the most attention. Created by a local artist who signed his name as "Schasstein," three-dimensional murals, known by the French term trompe l'oeil, were painted on the mansion's walls and many of its ceilings. In the main hall, Schasstein created columns, statues and vases, all seemingly three-dimensional. More await in the library, where 3-D tassels surround the ceiling, framing cornices, mouldings and more murals.

In 1988, the castle and its grounds were sold to a developer and its contents auctioned. But as so often happens in small communities, the local residents were not about to let their most prominent building disappear. In 1993, the Township of Wilmot bought the property and began restoration. By holding a celebrity auction, they were able to recover many of the original contents, including an old toy collection. New municipal offices were added to the back of the building, and the interior was brought up to museum standards. A gift shop and washrooms were also added (although the original two-hole brick outhouse still stands outside).

Thanks largely to the remarkable murals, Parks Canada has declared the building a National Historic Site.

The castle is located on Regional Road 1. Baden lies on Regional Road 1, 18 kilometres west of Kitchener.

51

Castle Kilbride is a Baden landmark.

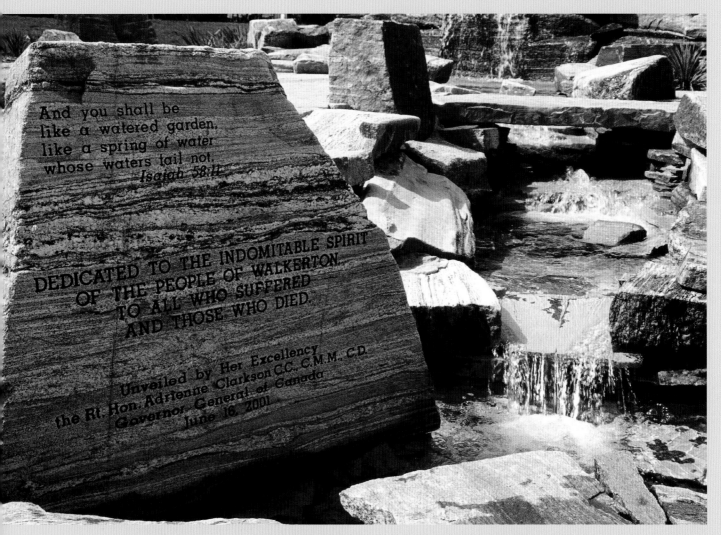

52

And you shall be
like a watered garden,
like a spring of water
whose waters fail not.
Isaiah 58:11

DEDICATED TO THE INDOMITABLE SPIRIT
OF THE PEOPLE OF WALKERTON.
TO ALL WHO SUFFERED
AND THOSE WHO DIED.

Unveiled by Her Excellency
the Rt. Hon. Adrienne Clarkson C.C. C.M.M. C.D.
Governor General of Canada
June 16, 2001

Walkerton's memorial fountain recalls the tragedy of the tainted water that killed seven residents and hospitalized much of the farming town's population.

Death from the Tap
Walkerton's Memorial of Tragedy

May 12, 2000, was a torrential spring day. Heavy rains poured down on the cattle farms that surround the Bruce County town of Walkerton. As the raindrops joined into trickles and then into streams, the water washed over the cow droppings and plunged into the town's water wells. Normally, the treatment applied to drinking water would render the polluted water harmless.

Five days later, town residents began to suffer wrenching cramps, fever and bloody diarrhea. Within a week they began to die. Two weeks after the deluge, more than 150 people were in hospital and another 500 were sick. By the time the epidemic was over, seven people had died and 2,300 taken ill.

Taking much of the blame for the disaster was the controversial government of Premier Mike Harris, whose policy had been to cut or privatize many services, including the regulation of municipal water quality and the enforcement of safe-water guidelines. But the main culprits were the town's own water-management staff, who had failed to use the proper doses of chlorine and routinely neglected to monitor the quality of the water pouring from the town's taps.

The tragedy sparked an extensive commission of inquiry headed by Justice Dennis O'Connor, a book, a CBC news special and construction of a memorial.

When the epidemic struck, the town was in the process of creating a heritage garden dedicated to the community's history. Following the deaths, Harry Jongerden, head gardener for the popular Stratford Festival, expanded the design to incorporate a water memorial dedicated to the victims. Donations poured in until $140,000 had been raised; volunteers from the town and several surrounding communities offered their labour. Seven heritage plaques now line a path that winds past the gardens and leads to a commemorative fountain with a memorial plaque that reads, "Dedicated to the indomitable spirit of the people of Walkerton, to all who suffered and those who died."

On June 16, 2001, a year after the deadly outbreak, Canada's then governor general, Adrienne Clarkson, stepped before a crowd of more than one thousand people and praised the community "for putting on a brave face in the throes of heartache and pain" and for their determination to look to the future.

The memorial garden lies at the south end of Walkerton near the corner of First Street and Yonge.

THE ST. THOMAS TRAIN STATION

53

Ontario's Longest Small Town Station

THE VAST FIELD of weeds gives scant indication that here once sprawled southwestern Ontario's most extensive rail yards. In 1873, a railway line known as the Canada Southern Railway (CSR), in reality an American-owned shortcut between Buffalo and Michigan, selected St. Thomas as a major divisional yard and repair facility. It lay halfway along the Ontario portion of its line. Beside the yards, the CSR added engine shops and a stunning railway station.

Although only 12 metres wide, the brick building stretched 120 metres along the tracks. Inside were offices for the general superintendent, paymaster, solicitor and freight agents as well as sleeping quarters for the train crews and the station's restaurant staff. On the ground floor were the restaurant and waiting rooms for the passengers. Italianate in style, the station was designed by a local contractor named Edgar Berryman. The building used 400,000 bricks and contained eight chimneys. Each end boasted four pilasters that led to a temple-like gable. A row of fifty windows lined the upper floor, while the ground level was broken by two archways. The station was the only one in Ontario that was segregated, not for the passengers but for the train crews, whose quarters were racially separated.

It was here in 1885 that one of North America's most notable railway accidents

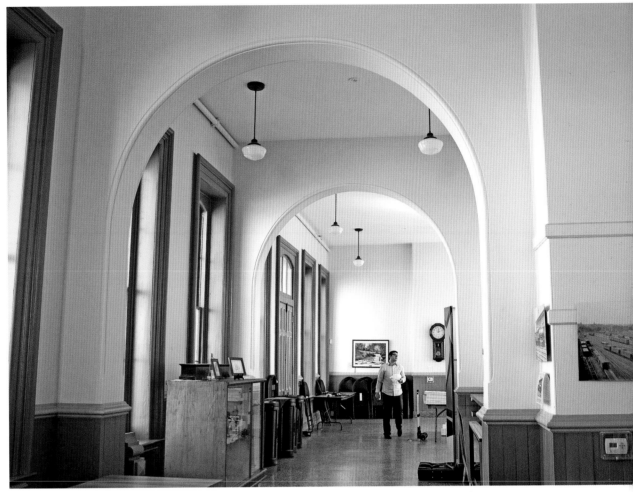

The interior of the historic St. Thomas railway station has been restored and now houses the North America Railway Hall of Fame. Opposite: The restored St. Thomas station faces the home of the Elgin County Railroad Museum.

occurred, when the famous Barnum & Bailey circus elephant, Jumbo, was killed in the face of a sudden and unexpected onrushing freight train. A statue in the town recalls the story.

Across the wide yard full of tracks and sidings, the repair shops were the largest in the region. But by 1968 the rail line had become part of Penn Central and then Conrail, before being incorporated into the Canadian National Railway. But the line duplicated existing trackage, and the company closed down the operation.

Eventually, it removed all the tracks to the dismay of the Elgin County Railway Museum, which continues to offer one of the most extensive collections of historic railway rolling stock in Ontario.

Thanks to On Track St. Thomas and the North America Railway Hall of Fame, the building has been preserved and restored and now serves as an event venue, offices and a gallery of Hall of Fame inductees including singer/songwriter Gordon Lightfoot, composer of "The Canadian Railroad Trilogy."

NORMANDALE
Ontario's First Iron-Making Capital

ASK ANYONE WHERE Ontario's iron industry began, and the answer would more than likely be Hamilton. But Hamilton was a relative latecomer to that industry. Instead, pioneers wanted their needs to be close at hand, and for that reason much of Ontario's early iron-making took place near the larger peat bogs. When burned in a furnace, bog ore produces iron, which can then be moulded into such needed items as stoves, plough shares and axes.

One of Ontario's first such iron furnaces began operation on the shore of Lake Erie in a community called Normandale. In 1810, an English ironmaster named John Mason erected a small furnace on the banks of a small creek that flowed into Lake Erie. He soon sold the operation to Joseph Van Norman who, along with Hiram Capron and George Tillson, expanded the operation to include a 30-metre-high brick chimney, a water wheel and a pair of bellows.

The town that grew around the operation took its name from Van Norman. At its peak, Normandale could count four hundred residents. But by 1840, with the supply of timber and bog ore depleted, Van Norman moved to Marmora, where he launched another iron-making industry, and Normandale became a ghost town. The small harbour could not sustain larger fishing vessels, and it soon silted in.

But the place wouldn't remain a true ghost town, as cottagers and those preferring a rural lifestyle began to build along the old village streets. Enough remains of old Normandale to warrant a visit. Mill Street still leads past the site of the furnace and is a trail to the beach. At the main intersection of Normandale Road and Main Street, the Union Hotel, built in the 1840s, still stands — now carefully restored. Adjacent to it is the former post office, with its "boom town" facade. Further along the main street is a regency cottage–style stone residence with its cupola and wraparound porch and French doors, built by Van Norman's son, Romaine.

Many other early buildings mix with the newer homes in this historic gully, where the ghosts of the town's early days yet lurk.

54

The former Union Hotel in the near "ghost town" of Normandale dates from the town's iron-making days in the early 1800s.

WROXETER

A "Former Ghost Town" Brought Back to Life

IN WHAT MUST be Ontario's most unusual village entrance sign, that at Wroxeter announces that you are about to enter a "former ghost town."

That unusual distinction arose from an entry in a much earlier book by this author, entitled *Ghost Towns of Ontario*. The inclusion related to the main street of this leafy riverside village, where fifteen of the eighteen business establishments were at that time boarded up.

In an era when main streets grew around the water power of a nearby stream and when transportation between such communities was slow and muddy, shops catering to every need abounded. Hotels, general stores, harness makers, butchers and bakers all operated out of separate establishments. Wroxeter was no exception and, by 1874, twenty businesses flourished along the main street. Industries included four mills and a furniture factory. An influx of seasonal workers briefly gave the settlement the population it needed to become an incorporated village.

But thanks to the water power supplied by the Maitland River, other villages began to grow as well—places like Fordwich, Gorrie and, especially, Wingham, all enjoying a location on the Toronto, Grey & Bruce Railway. Then, with the shift of grain-growing to western Canada and the closing of the rail lines, many villages declined. The auto age and improved roads shifted business to Wingham, and the stores and businesses on Wroxeter's main streets closed one by one, until by the 1980s nearly all were shuttered.

But Wroxeter, despite the spectral appearance of the commercial core, was no ghost town—as the three hundred or so residents can attest. The dubious exposure provided the impetus to greatly improve not just the main street, but the river area as well. And to celebrate its revitalized heritage, the community inaugurated a "ghost town" hoedown.

Wroxeter is still pretty quiet, and most residents still go to Wingham to shop. But today, the community is true to its roadside sign, which proudly declares that it is truly now a *former* ghost town.

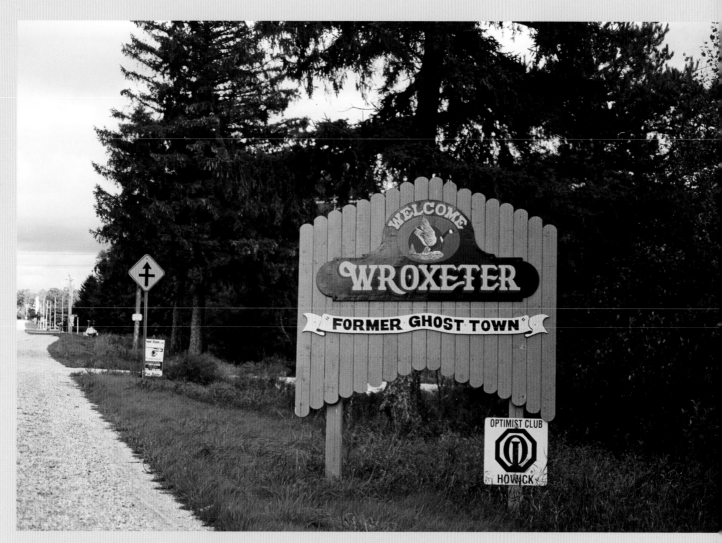

55

After being included in a book about ghost towns, the residents of this western Ontario town reclaimed their community, proclaiming it a "former" ghost town.

RUTHVEN
A Mansion in a Ghost Town

RUTHVEN PARK IS a "castle" in a real ghost town. The village of Indiana was, throughout much of the nineteenth century, a bustling mill town that grew up around the mills on the Grand River.

As the banks of the Grand River began to fill with settlers, William Hamilton Merritt, chief promoter of the Welland Canal, began to push for a canal that would link the settlements of the Lower Grand River. One of Merritt's contractors, David Thompson, arrived at lock station one and built two grist mills, a carding mill, a lumber mill and a distillery. The town of Indiana was laid out and, at its peak, could claim more than four hundred residents. A short distance away Thompson built a grand mansion, which he called Ruthven Park.

Built of Indiana limestone between 1845 and 1847, the thirty-six-room structure overlooked the river. Four columns soared the full two storeys to mark the main riverside entrance. Inside were two black marble fireplaces and an oval staircase to the second floor. Surrounding the mansion was Thompson's 450-hectare farm.

By the 1870s, the railways had arrived and the canal fell into disuse. The wooden lock gates rotted and the locks filled with debris. Indiana became a ghost town and, by 1900, would count fewer than two dozen inhabitants. But the mansion remained in the family.

In 1994, the federal government declared the building a national historic site and the property was deeded by the family to the Lower Grand River Land Trust, which has undertaken not just the restoration of the mansion but also the conservation of the lands around it. Summer students have excavated the ghost town itself and restored the large Catholic cemetery, which over the years had become heavily overgrown. Of the town, only a pair of buildings survives on the now largely vanished grid network of roads.

The Land Trust leads tours through the mansion, which is located on Highway 54 between the towns of Caledonia and Cayuga.

56

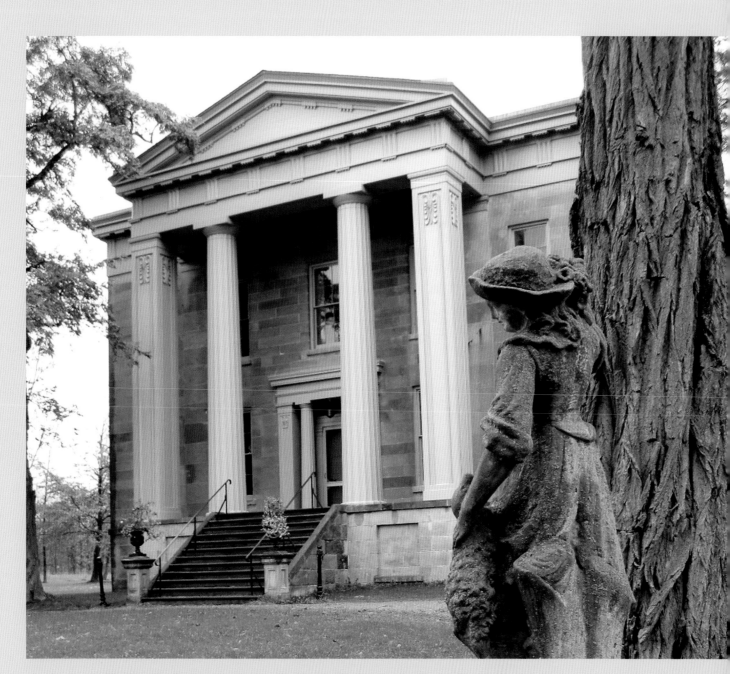

The grand mansion known as Ruthven Park is almost the only remaining structure in the ghost town of Indiana near Cayuga.

57

Port Dover's "ghost" mausoleum has long been a roadside curiosity.

PORT DOVER'S GHOST MAUSOLEUM

MANY ARE THE times that the traveller will quickly discern from the window of a car an eye-catching feature. On Highway 6 west of Port Dover, it's a thing of curiosity — for there, on the north side of the road, stands a peculiar structure. Its columns rise above the overgrown field, with no seeming neighbour or sign to explain what it may be.

The sad structure is in fact a lonely mausoleum built by the Port Dover Cemetery Board in the hopes of encouraging some of the area's wealthier residents to consider interring their deceased loved ones in elegant, and costly, surroundings.

But the cost, $225 to $275 per crypt, did not seem worth the expense in 1927. With its four Doric columns, the entrance was grand enough. Even the evocative words in the ad for the facility could not attract any business: "No matter how inclement the weather, the entrance halls of our mausoleum present a beautiful chapel."

But no takers arrived, and the concrete building remained vacant. It did, however, attract the attention of a Toronto filmmaker. It was here in 2008 that Internext Studios chose to film three scenes from its science fiction movie, *Six Reasons Why*, starring Canadian actor Colm Feore.

Port Dover is well known for considerably more than the abandoned mausoleum. Its long sandy beach and fish food restaurants keep the lakeside town busy most of the year. And whenever a Friday the 13th rolls around, so, too, do the motorcycles. That date has become a call to thousands of motorcycle enthusiasts from across Canada and the United States, making Port Dover the site of some of North America's premier motorcycle rallies.

PARIS PLAINS STONE CHURCH

NTARIO'S CITIES AND countryside contain many magnificent stone buildings, from the huge blocks of red sandstone that form the Queens Park legislative buildings and the old city hall, both in Toronto, to the rubble stone that hardened pioneers gathered from the fields to make

the handsome St. Margaret's Church on the Bruce Peninsula. But no stone construction technique is as distinctive or as delightful as the neat rows of cobblestones on the Paris Plains Church near the intersection of Brant County roads 24A and 28, north of Paris, Ontario.

When Levi Boughton migrated from Rochester, New York, to Paris in the late 1840s, he brought with him a construction technique that few Upper Canadians had

ever before seen. Originally devised by the ancient Romans during their occupation of England, it was a technique that could utilize common fieldstones, the bane of many farmers in the Paris and Brantford area, to create buildings of rare beauty.

The technique involved gathering thousands of field stones, usually dolomite or limestone, that had been relentlessly ground into spheres by the great glaciers and the swirling of their meltwaters. The stones would then be passed through a standard ring to ensure uniformity of shape and size. Then they would be laid in level "courses" to construct the walls of the buildings. The result was walls of incredibly uniform rows of cobblestones, almost as if they had been handmade.

The contractor for the church, and about a dozen other buildings in the town of Paris itself, was Philo Hull. Here, the technique was applied to a church, fences and several houses of different dimensions, making Paris the centre of this style. Later in the century, when brickmaking made construction so much cheaper, Boughton's cobblestone style died completely. Occasionally it is resurrected in individual homes, not because it is cheaper, but because of its rare beauty and grace. But back in Boughton's day, it was an inventive way to turn a nuisance into a thing of beauty.

58

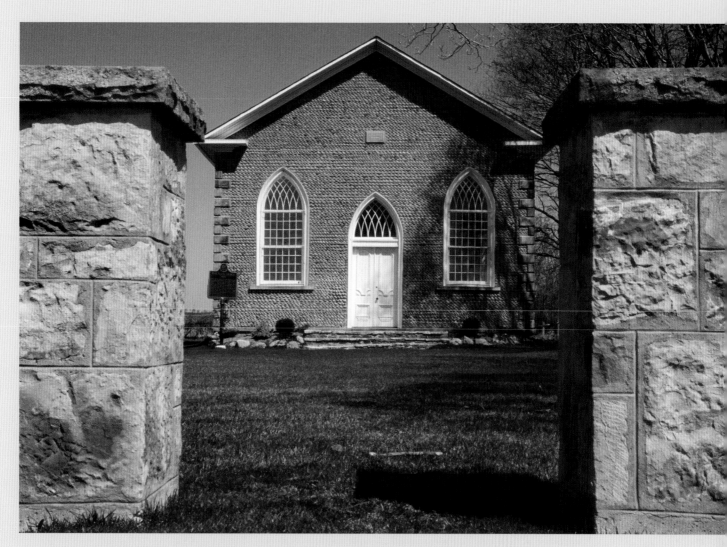

The unusual cobblestone walls on the Paris Plains Church near Brantford.

THE MAGICAL CYPRUS LAKE GROTTO

59

THE TIMELESS AND irresistible forces of nature sometimes create magical landscapes. Few people enter a cave to go diving. Yet within the boundaries of one of Ontario's newest national parks, the Bruce Peninsula National Park, cave swimmers can dive into waters 12 metres deep. The grotto, at 20 metres long, ranges in width from 9 to 12 metres and looks out onto a small cove surrounded by rugged grey cliffs and a beach of broken boulders. Its isolation, its rugged beauty, and the tranquility of a turquoise blue lagoon, make the setting almost magical.

For tens of thousands of years, the waves of Georgian Bay relentlessly pounded away at the limestone cliffs of the Bruce Peninsula. Deep inside, rainwater crept through cracks in the limestone to dissolve the rock from within. The result is a shoreline of cliffs, caves, the unusual rock pillars known as "flowerpots," and the Cyprus Lake Grotto. This outstanding assembly of unusual natural features, along with many rare species of flora and fauna, has long made the peninsula a popular destination for hikers and nature lovers.

Over the years, however, the lack of public land has hindered access for most. To remedy this, Parks Canada created a new national park to allow Canadians to experience one of their nation's great natural wonders. Local politics and hostility, however, prevented the park from taking in the entire northern peninsula. As a result, Bruce Peninsula National Park consists of three unconnected segments. The Fathom Five segment is set aside for divers to explore the underwater caves and shipwrecks, Flowerpot Island contains the best examples of these towering limestone pillars, while the Cypress Lake segment contains the grotto and shoreline.

Beside the grotto, trails lead to overhanging cliffs, underground passages and natural caves. The park is located on Highway 6 between Wiarton and Tobermory.

Limestone pillars known as "flowerpots" in Bruce Peninsula National Park.

LAKE ERIE'S COLD WAR SUBMARINE

HMCS *Ojibwa*

LAKE ERIE'S HERITAGE is decidedly maritime. Numerous little coves evolved into busy fishing ports, many of which are still active. Shipwrecks abound as do marine museums. But the last thing one would expect to find on the Lake Erie shore is a real Cold War submarine.

Launched in 1964 as the HMS *Onyx*, an Oberon-class submarine, the HMCS *Ojibwa* served as a Canadian Cold War sub under the Marine Forces Atlantic until 1997.

Submerged, the *Ojibwa* could attain speeds in excess of 30 kilometres per hour and could remain with its crew of up to seventy-five submariners submerged for fifty-six days. Although it carried twenty-four torpedoes, each 6 metres long, none was fired in hostile action. Its only confrontation came with a Spanish fishing vessel caught fishing illegally in Canadian waters during what was known as the "Turbot War."

Cramped sleeping quarters could accommodate forty-two submariners, twenty-four at a time, although when needed crew might sleep in the torpedo room. Crew members would often share sleeping bags even though they might not wash for up to three months at a time. To pass the time, crew would enjoy games of cribbage or chess, or watch movies projected on a sheet. The *Ojibwa* ended its service in 1997 and

was decommissioned the following year. Its proposed fate: the scrapyard.

While looking for a tank for its museum display, the Elgin County Military Museum in St. Thomas saw in the sub an opportunity to celebrate the Canadian Navy's 100th anniversary in 2010, and discussions began in 2008 with the Ministry of National Defence to purchase and move the *Ojibwa*. But negotiations dragged on longer than expected (no surprise there), as did the finalizing of techniques required to move the vessel from Halifax — 1,200 nautical miles up the St. Lawrence River and through the locks of the St. Lawrence Seaway and the Welland Canal — without damage to the sub or the locks. Towing was not an option. To solve the problem a floating dry dock was constructed to carry the *Ojibwa* to its resting place in June 2012. Tours began a year later.

Resting on the river bank below Port Burwell's historic wooden lighthouse, the shiny black hulk extends nearly 90 metres long, while the distance from the hull to the top of the conning tower is equivalent to a five-storey building.

Canada has had submarines as far back as 1913, but the *Ojibwa* was the first to be owned by the Canadian Navy, one of five. In 2014, the Museum of Naval History will open beside the submarine itself.

60

An unlikely place to find a Cold War-era Canadian submarine
is on the shores of Lake Erie at Port Burwell

THE GHOST SQUIRRELS OF EXETER

61

A WHITE APPARITION SCAMPERS across the grass and leaps into a tree. No, it is not a Halloween prank, nor is it an optical illusion. Rather it is one of Exeter's white squirrels.

First reported by local hunters in 1912, the white squirrels in this south-western Ontario town have become a tourist attraction in a prosperous community that can claim few tourist draws.

In fact, the town has gone to great lengths to adopt the furry ball of white. In 2001, council passed a bylaw prohibiting the harming or hunting of wild squirrels. And the town's Business Improvement Area has incorporated the animal as its logo. So, even if you don't see any white squirrels in the town parks or neighbourhood yards, you can spot them on street signs, trash receptacles and town banners. And while you can't take one home with you, you can drop in to the visitor centre at the south end of the main street and purchase white squirrel key chains, fluffy dolls, earrings or candles.

According to Ontario biologists, the critters are not albinos as one might initially assume, nor are they a separate species. Rather, they are a genetic variation of the more common grey squirrel but with different amounts of melanin. The town is said to have more than a hundred of the animals.

But Exeter is not North America's only home to the white squirrel. This author has witnessed white squirrels in the eastern Ontario community of Chaffeys Locks, and populations exist in Olney, Illinois, and in Brevard, North Carolina.

West of downtown Toronto, a small group of white squirrels inhabits Trinity-Bellwoods Park on Queen Street West, but in fact they are true albinos with the typical pink eyes. A nearby Queen Street West coffee shop displays an image of the white squirrel.

Exeter is situated on Highway 4, about an hour north of London.

An unusual population of white squirrels finds a home in the parks and yards of Exeter. (Photo by David Bishop, supplied courtesy of the Exeter BIA.)

The Town of Exeter's Business Improvement Area has incorporated the resident white squirrels in their logos and street furniture.

CENTRAL ONTARIO & TORONTO AREA

Central Ontario & Toronto Area

Georgian Bay

Midland
100
75 12

Collingwood

63
Barrie
89
94

Lake Simcoe

24

400

62
Orangeville
9
95
78

Newmarket

67
Uxbridge

404

88

68

76

71

92
401

Bowmanville
93

86

10

70
Guelph

401

84
Milton
66

Toronto
Markham
85

401
102 90

83 79

81 72

82 91

87 73

6

QEW
97 80, 74
Lake Ontario

101

QEW

Brantford

403

65

54

3

Hamilton
96

Grimsby

QEW
St. Catharines

77

64 98

Pt. Colborne
Fort Erie
69

99

Lake Ontario

N

Map not to scale

Lake Erie

THE SWAMP THAT FEEDS THE WORLD
The Amazing Holland Marsh

LIKE MUCH THAT is interesting in Ontario, the Holland Marsh is paid scant attention by travellers. To most, the marsh is little more than the flat, black fields that flash past along Highway 400. Yet, for the driver who exits at Canal Road, the marsh becomes one of the most interesting bits of landscape, not just in Ontario, but in Canada. It is the country's largest vegetable garden.

That wasn't the case around the turn of the twentieth century, when this post-glacial lake bed, with decayed plants 30 metres deep, was good for little else than growing marsh grasses to stuff into mattresses. Then, in 1904, a Bradford grocer named Watson convinced professor W. H. Day of the Ontario Agricultural College in Guelph to investigate the possibility of draining the swamp for vegetable production. All his studies and experiments pointed to the same thing—the swamp could become one of Canada's premier market-gardens.

In 1925, the Ontario Department of Agriculture began to drain the bog. Canals and dikes enclosed both sides of the wide valley like huge brackets, diverting the water to Lake Simcoe.

By 1930, the rich black soil was drained and ready for farming. The first farmers to arrive were eighteen Dutch families from

A view across the Holland Marsh as harvest season approaches.

Hamilton, Ontario, in 1934. Many others, including Russians and Poles, followed, and within a few years the one-time swamp had become one of North America's leading vegetable-producing areas. (The name "Holland" does not come from the Dutch settlers, but rather from Major A. Holland, the British surveyor who laid out the land in 1830.)

Canal Road, which skirts the northern rim of the marsh, provides the best look at the 2,900-hectare marsh. From Highway 9 to Yonge Street in Bradford, Canal Road follows the northerly of the two canals through a world of overhanging willows and still canal waters. It passes sprawling modern backsplits that contrast with the cabins and trailers that house the seasonal workers who pick the lettuce, potatoes, celery, parsnips, cabbage, cauliflower and the 120,000 tonnes of carrots that sprout each year from the fertile earth.

SIZE MATTERS
The Battle over the Country's Smallest Jail

FOR MANY YEARS, tourist brochures for the village of Tweed boasted of its having North America's smallest jail. The little stone lockup, then serving as a tourist information centre, measured a mere 4.9 metres by 6.1 metres. And for years the claim went unchallenged. Then several other communities began to discover that they, too, had little heritage jails, sometimes literally in their own backyards.

Creemore jumped in with its jail of 4.5 metres by 6.0 metres. Located beside the library, a block east of the main street, it now serves as a museum. The tiny cells remain as they were when they held the local town drunk (or, in one case, a cow).

Down a small side street in Coboconk, a little stone building was scheduled for demolition. A local seniors' group lobbied for its preservation, and so the "Coby" jail was saved. Its dimensions, however, proved to be a few centimetres shorter than that in Creemore, and today it functions as a gift shop run by the same seniors' group.

Deep in south-western Ontario, the little railway town of Rodney also has its own tiny claim to fame—a brick jail beside the fairgrounds that measures a mere 4.5 metres by 5.4 metres. After serving as a book drop for many years, it is now a tourist information centre, although only seldom open.

Port Dalhousie, near St. Catharines, was not to be outdone and submitted its own candidate with measurements almost identical to those of the Rodney jail. It is now part of a bar. Also, almost forgotten, and unacclaimed, is the former jail in Providence Bay on Manitoulin Island, which is now converted to a cabin for tourists.

But the smallest of them all, and virtually inaccessible, is the one-cell lockup in the ghost town of Barens River. A short-lived gold-mining town, it lies on an isolated lake far to the north of Red Lake, and is accessible only by float plane.

And as for the original claimant in Tweed—it's now back in business as a community police station!

63

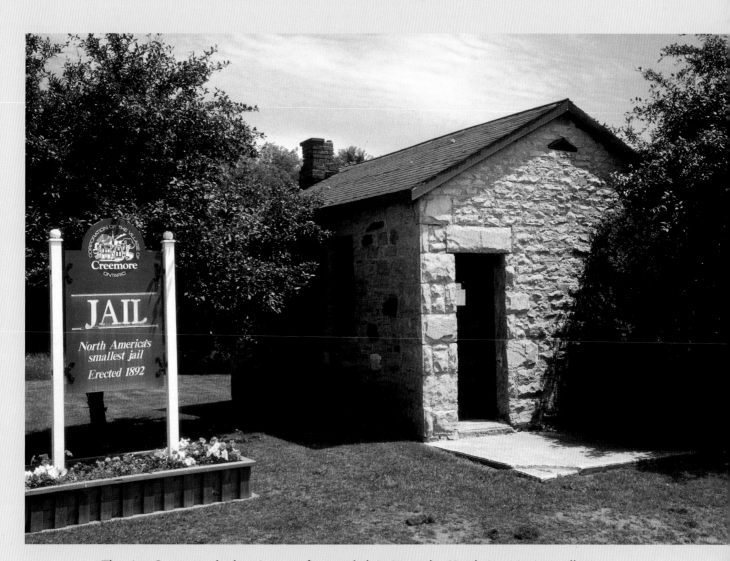

The tiny Creemore lockup is one of several claiming to be North America's smallest.

THE COMFORT GIANT 64
Canada's Biggest Sugar Maple Tree

ONE SPECIMEN OF the tree that symbolizes Canada may be older than the nation itself. The Comfort Maple squats wide and solid beside a field near Welland, Ontario. It had been there for three hundred years when, in 1816, the Comfort family first settled the land. And there it has remained, its survival defying all the odds.

Ontario once boasted a magnificent forest cover. Oak, hemlock, beech and maple provided a cooling leafy canopy that assured a high water table, which in turn allowed the many rivers and streams to flow year-round — cascading streams that powered the countless pioneer mills. But that forest quickly vanished, for what fire and old age didn't claim, pioneer wood hewers did.

With the forest gone, the water table lowered and the streams dried up, turning the once-vibrant mill towns into ghost towns. But the Comfort Maple survived. With its girth of 8 metres and crown width of 28 metres, the 30-metre-high giant became a local attraction, and owner Earl Hampton Comfort set aside a piece of land solely for the preservation of his tree. In 1961, his sister Edna donated the tree and 4 hectares of land around it to the Niagara Region Conservation Authority.

Today the authority maintains about a half hectare of land, a parking lot, and a few benches. As the ancient tree ages, it has become necessary to support some of the branches with guy wires. The tree sits on Metler Road, west of Victoria Avenue, which leads south from Exit 57 on the Queen Elizabeth Way.

The Comfort Maple is said to be Canada's largest sugar maple.

CHIEFSWOOD
The Poet's Two-Sided Palace

OVERLOOKING ONTARIO'S historic Grand River, looms one of the area's most unusual mansions. Known as Chiefswood and home to legendary Canadian poet Pauline Johnson, it contains two front doors and no back door. Both facades — the front and the back — of the handsome building are identical.

Pauline Johnson's father, George Johnson, was an important chief of the Mohawks of the Six Nations. Overcoming family objections, he married an American woman, Emily Howell.

Shortly after their marriage, he built a fine mansion for his wife and future family. High on a bank overlooking the swirling waters of the wide Grand River, a route busy with not only Indian canoes but barges and schooners plying the Grand River canal, he built Chiefswood. It was a fine two-storey structure, unlike the log or wattle cabins most of the population inhabited. Doors were centred on both the side of the house that faced the river and on the opposite side, which faced the road.

The door facing the river was to accommodate the traditions of his Mohawk kin, who travelled by river, while the door facing the road was for the convenience of his wife's English friends and family, who travelled by road. It was probably Canada's first multicultural domicile.

It was in this unusual abode that Pauline Johnson was born and later started school. Despite a mere seven years of formal studies, she read constantly, absorbing works by Shakespeare, Milton and Scott. When George Johnson died in 1884, Pauline Johnson's family could no longer afford Chiefswood and moved into the nearby city of Brantford. There she began to write poems for publication in the local *Brantford Expositor*.

Soon Johnson began to appear before audiences to recite such poems as "Cry from an Indian Wife" and "The Song My Paddle Sings." Displaying an uncanny sense of the stage, she performed in both English and Indian costume and displayed such articles as hunting knives, animal pelts and — a grotesque choice — human scalps.

For seventeen years, Johnson toured North America and Europe, finally settling in Vancouver. There, sadly, she succumbed to breast cancer and died in 1913.

To commemorate the famous poet, Pauline Johnson's birth home was made a historic site. Now a museum, it is open for visits and tours. Inside, the simple furniture of the day is on display, and the exibits tell the story of the poet herself and the story of the mansion with two front doors.

This historic site overlooks the Grand River on County Road 54, 12 kilometres east of Brantford.

65

Pauline Johnson's home, Chiefswood, has two front doors but no back door, to accommodate the cultures of her mixed Mohawk and English parentage.

DWARF CEDARS 66
Ontario's Oldest Trees

THINK OF AN old-growth forest and you think of redwood trees that soar upward until their tops disappear in a canopy of green. You don't envisage gnarly little cedars that twist out of the side of a rock and extend only 3 or 4 metres into the air. Yet these spindly little survivors are Ontario's oldest trees.

Normally a swamp species, the eastern white cedars are found along the lip of the Niagara Escarpment, some of them dating back more than six hundred years, and one nearly a thousand years. Dating such a tree is not an easy job. It requires boring into the trunk and then counting, often with the aid of a microscope, the hundreds of nearly invisible rings concentrated into the span of a hand.

Starting as seeds lodged in the limestone crevices centuries ago, the saplings edged slowly outward and then bent upward to face the warm and nutritious sunlight. Anchored in the stony depths, with no soil to feed them, the trees grew imperceptibly. But at least they grew. Their inaccessible location on the side of the cliff spared them from loggers, farmers and browsing animals, and even from the encroachment of other tree species. While original forests were falling all across Canada, the sturdy little white cedars sat firm and continued their slow growth skyward.

Thanks to the creation of a series of provincial parks, and a UNESCO designation as a World Biosphere Reserve, much of the Niagara Escarpment is finally available to the public. One of the best sites from which to view the ancient trees is in the conservation area at Rattlesnake Point. A short path leads from the parking area to the trail along the brink, where a stone fence protects careless walkers from a dangerous and likely deadly tumble over the precipice.

The trees can be identified by their light green, flat cedar needles, and by their trademark origin in the side of the cliff face. But as for the age of those that you see, only a bore sample and tedious tally of the tiny rings can tell you if the tree is sixty or six hundred years old.

A good location to view the gnarled old cedars is in Rattlesnake Point Conservation Area off Derry Road, west of Milton.

Ontario's oldest trees are also among its smallest.

Ontario's Taj Mahal
The Thomas Foster Memorial

You don't need to spend a lot of time looking for this one; it dominates the countryside on County Road 1 about 5 kilometres north of Uxbridge. Thomas Foster was born near Toronto in 1852 and moved to the hamlet of Leaskdale, north of Uxbridge, where he ran the local hotel. He later moved back to Toronto, where he was elected a member of Parliament and later mayor of the city. One of his oddest acts was to offer a prize to the woman who could bear the most children in a ten-year period. He made his fortune by investing in real estate.

Following the death of his wife, he travelled the world. While visiting India he gazed in wonder at the beautiful Taj Mahal, built in 1628 by Shah Jahan as a monument to his wife, Mumtaz Mahal. Foster decided that he, too, would build a Taj-like temple for his own wife. The location he chose was a hilltop just north of Uxbridge and not far from his home town of Leaskdale.

In 1934 he commissioned architects J. H. Craig and H. H. Madill to design the memorial. Workers cleared away the hilltop and then began carefully laying limestone and marble according to the intricate plan. When they were done, the strange Byzantine monument rose more than 18 metres into the air. The onion dome was built of copper and allowed the sun to filter through twelve stained-glass windows. The coloured rays fell upon marble mosaics, lighting up the pink, green and black inlays on the walls and floor. Surrounding the floor are marble pillars, each different from the other. Against one wall stand the three crypts: his, that of his wife, and the third containing his daughter.

Maintained by the Foster Memorial Committee, and designated as a heritage building, the memorial plays host to weddings and plays, and is open to the public on the first and third Sunday of each month through the summer.

67

Thomas Foster modelled his memorial to his wife after India's Taj Mahal.

BELFOUNTAIN PARK 68
The Stamp Man's Legacy

UNDER THE GAZE of a small cannon, the west branch of the Credit River plunges over a 10-metre waterfall and then tumbles down a rocky canyon. Beside the cannon are winding pathways lined with elaborate stonework, a chapel-like cave with the name Yellowstone, and a stone fountain with a bell on top.

This is the Belfountain Conservation Area. The creation of millionaire philanthropist Charles W. Mack, it is one of Ontario's most unusual parks. Better known as the industrialist who invented and then manufactured the cushion stamp, Mack purchased this property on the rocky bank of the Credit River in 1908. Here, by the site of an early grist mill and quarry, he built a summer home for himself and his wife, and they named it Luck-e-nuf. He then hired master landscaper Sam Brock to create a park.

When finished, Brock had created a wonderland in stone. His park contained a dam for swimming, a lookout point, and a cave that he had converted into a chapel-like room. He had slung a suspension bridge across the canyon and topped it all off with a stone fountain with a bell on top, to commemorate the name of the village.

Belfountain, which lines the canyon rim, began in 1825 as a pioneer settlement named McCurdy's Village. During the 1860s it became home to mining company executives who managed the stone quarries in the Credit Canyon below. By the time Mack showed up, the mines had closed, and the miners' villages of Brimstone and Forks of the Credit had become ghost towns.

But Mack's park was quite popular, for when he had finished it, he opened the grounds to the public. Visitors could come to picnic, hike or swim, provided that they obeyed Charles Mack's rules: no swimming on Sundays, and men were to wear swim tops and women skirts at all times.

After Mack's death in 1943, his park was sold and operated as a commercial business until 1955, when the Credit Valley Conservation Authority purchased the property. Additional acquisitions between 1961 and 1973 have given the grounds more space for picnicking and hiking trails.

Although Mack's modest cottage and cabin have been reduced to their foundations, most of Brock's handiwork remains in place. You can look into the Yellowstone cave, watch the waterfall from the lookout, cross the canyon on a bridge, or simply sit by the fountain with the bell on top.

The park lies in the village of Belfountain on the Forks of the Credit Road.

Beautiful Belfountain Park was once a private estate.

Beautiful Point Abino Lighthouse

PERHAPS IT IS because most of them lie on isolated shorelines, out of view of most landlubbers, that lighthouses are among the least appreciated of Ontario's heritage structures.

Some are small and squat, made of wood; others are tall and elegant, constructed of stone or brick. Then there is the lighthouse at Point Abino. Built of poured concrete, it is unlike any other lighthouse in Ontario. Constructed in a form of architecture known as Greek Revival, it is easily the most elegant lighthouse along the Ontario side of the Great Lakes.

Point Abino is located on Lake Erie just west of Fort Erie. With the urban boom that engulfed southern Ontario and upper New York State in the late 1800s, increasing numbers of city dwellers sought out the beaches and breezes of the nearest lakeshores. These numbers swelled following the opening of the Peace Bridge between Buffalo and Fort Erie in 1927. While more modest cottages and cabins crowded the beaches in nearby Crystal Beach, the forested peninsula at Point Abino became the exclusive enclave of wealthy industrialists. Families from New York and Ohio like the Rich family, owners of Rich products, and the Baird family, owners of the Buffalo News, erected grand summer homes here.

The lighthouse was completed in 1918, built to replace a light ship that was destroyed in a storm in 1913, killing all on board. A light-keeper's residence was added in 1921. Prior to the light ship, the dangerous shelf of rock, which creeps out from the point into

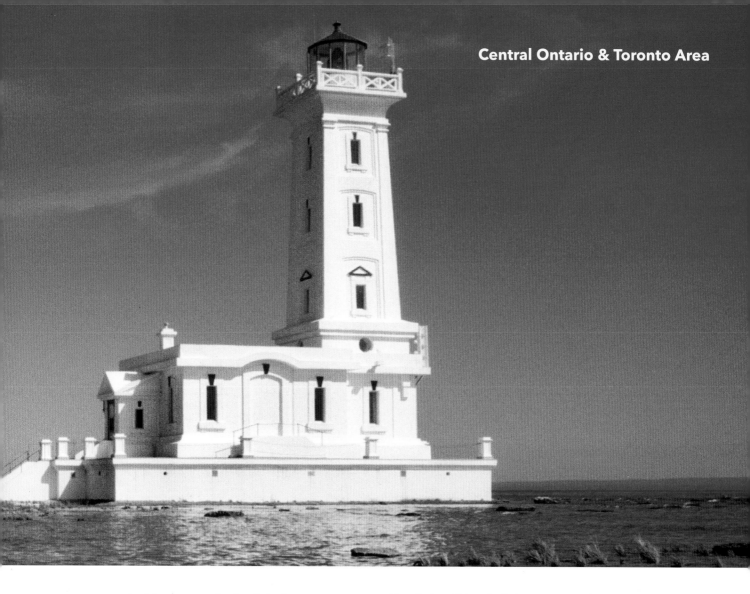

the lake, was marked only by buoys. Because the light was surrounded by water and private homes, the keepers had to access the dwelling by wading through the shallows.

Ontario has a rich lighthouse legacy. During the late 1800s the government built around the shores of Lake Huron half a dozen lofty stone structures that they termed the "Imperial Towers." Of the six, that at Cape Rich, near Southampton, is the most accessible. The squat stone lighthouse from the Duck Islands has been moved to the Mariners' Museum near Picton, Ontario. Port Rowan lays claim to having Ontario's oldest wooden lighthouse, and other lighthouses can be visited in Kincardine, on Long Point, in Prince Edward County, on the Toronto Islands, and at Wingfield Basin, near Tobermory. The province of Quebec

The Point Abino lighthouse is easily the most elegant on the Ontario shores of the Great Lakes.

also promotes a "lighthouse route" along the shores of the Lower St. Lawrence River.

Although no lighthouse in Ontario remains permanently staffed, most are still in use; the lighthouse at Point Abino was the last to be automated. The light has been declared a National Historic Site, and in 2001 was purchased by the town of Fort Erie. After being off-limits to non-residents, the structure can now be visited via a shuttle run by a volunteer organization, or on foot or by bike during designated hours.

The lighthouse and the property gate are located at the south end of Abino Road, 15 kilometres west of Fort Erie.

Rockwood's potholes.

Rockwood's Potholes

Most communities don't like to brag about their potholes, especially when they're 6 metres wide and 12 metres deep and number almost two hundred. Rockwood, Ontario, about 12 kilometres northeast of Guelph, is different. Residents not only boast of their potholes, but have created a park for them!

The reason for this pride is that the potholes are not a result of neglected roads, but are a fascinating creation of nature. Sedimentary rocks such as limestone or sandstone are among nature's softest. Easily eroded, they can be sculpted and washed by wind and water into a fairyland of shapes. Caves, natural bridges and rock pillars are but a few of the shapes that the rocks can assume.

Potholes are another form, occurring when boulders become trapped in the swirling eddies of fast-flowing rivers. As the boulders swirl around, they etch a hole in the bedrock beneath. Thousands of years must pass for the rocks to grind a hole even the size of a stew pot. Tens of thousands of years were required to form those at Rockwood.

This natural wonder is preserved in the Rockwood Conservation Area, on the western outskirts of the town. Trails lead from the parking lot up cliffs, past caves and even beside the ruins of a massive stone woollen mill and finally to the potholes themselves. Here, the Eramosa River flows though a watery labyrinth of potholes, some of which have collapsed, while others have eroded through. Other potholes remain high and dry and lurk darkly beneath the forest vegetation.

The most interesting way to explore them is to rent a canoe and coast lazily through the watery maze. You'll see potholes as you've never seen them before.

THE FLOATING MANSIONS OF LEMONVILLE

IT'S A WATERY wonderland, but one that's a long way from any river or lake. Lemonville sits on the slope of a sandy hill, the grey apartment towers and suburban glass offices of northeastern Toronto looming on the hazy horizon. An undistinguished hamlet that dates from pioneer days, Lemonville has seen a most unusual housing boom — mansions that float on water, or so they appear.

The water comes not from a river or a lake, but from a massive and mysterious underground reservoir. The ridge that looms behind the mansions is known as the Oak Ridges Moraine. A line of sandy hills, it was formed when the great glaciers that once covered Ontario cracked and began to melt. The icy meltwater carried sand and rocks into a long fissure in the ice, and by the time the glacier had melted, all that remained was the long ridge.

Because the soil in the hills is so porous, rainwater drains right through it, creating a high water table at the foot of the hills. That is not unusual, but the Lemonville area sits on a geological anomaly. While the water seeps quickly through the light, sandy upper soils of the ridge, the flow suddenly encounters a hard subsurface layer of clay. This propels it even faster toward the flats below and keeps the water near the surface like a massive underground lake contained only by the soil above it. Because of the downward force of the water in the hills behind, whenever the surface of the flats is broken, the water gushes upward like a geyser unleashed.

But house builders have turned what could have been a curse into a blessing. By digging carefully into the underground lake, they have landscaped the large housing lots into a miniature lake land. Surrounded by ponds, some more than a hectare in area, are mansions in styles that range from "California ranch" to "Woodbridge Italianate," or simply to "Scarborough suburban."

The land of the floating mansion extends south on McCowan Road for about a kilometre from Bethesda Road and 2 kilometres west along Bethesda Road to Kennedy Road.

71

Lemonville's mansions are set in a watery wonderland.

A Utilitarian Beauty   72
The R. C. Harris Filtration Plant

I N THE EAST end of Toronto, on a grassy slope overlooking Lake Ontario, sits one of the city's most attractive and least-known buildings—a filtration plant. Buildings housing public utilities seldom inspire either architectural elegance or public interest. But this one is different, and its difference is attributed to its namesake, Rowland Cole Harris.

Designed by Thomas Pomphrey, the building was constructed between 1932 and 1941. A second building was added in the early '50s. It was named after Harris, who was at the time Toronto's commissioner of works, and was a man who appreciated grand public buildings. The style that Harris chose for his filtration plant was Art Deco, an attractive modern style in vogue during the 1920s and '30s and often used for skyscrapers and other grand buildings.

Characterized by streamlined curves and shapes, Art Deco is also a style that was relatively short-lived. After the Second World War, the tastes of a generation railed against the recent past, the years of war and Depression. Architects moved to a simpler form known simply as the International style.

The R. C. Harris Filtration Plant occupies an extensive grassy park. The older structure, closer to the lake, is the pumping station, which draws water from over 2 kilometres out in the lake, while the higher building does the filtering and chlorinating.

While sleek lines dominate the exterior, herringbone tiles of marble imported from Siena decorate the foyer and vast halls. In these halls the plant can process 175 million gallons of water each day. Like the Distillery District, the R. C. Harris plant, which provides a modernistic set for movies, is popular with film companies.

While the public is free to wander the grounds, tours of the interior were halted following the September 11, 2001, attacks on the World Trade Center in New York. It was feared that a terrorist on such a tour might poison the city's water supply.

The plant is located on Queen Street East at Neville Park Boulevard, the eastern terminus of the Queen Street streetcar line. It also marks the eastern end of the popular Toronto neighbourhood known as the Beach, with its lakeside boardwalk, trendy cafés and eclectic mix of stores.

The Art Deco R. C. Harris sewage treatment plant.

An Industrial Survivor

Toronto's Gooderham and Worts Distillery District

73

ESPITE A HISTORY of insensitive and often unnecessary demolitions, Toronto can still claim a remarkable collection of heritage buildings. While structures like Old City Hall, Casa Loma and Union Station are widely known grand buildings, gritty industrial survivors are just as compelling and sometimes even more so.

Of paramount importance to Toronto's industrial heritage is the Gooderham and Worts complex at Parliament and Mill streets, in what was once the industrial heartland of east-end Toronto. Today it has been rechristened as "the Distillery District," and is Toronto's newest major tourist attraction. It is also considered Canada's oldest and most complete early-nineteenth-century industrial complex.

In the 1830s, English miller James Worts chose the confluence of the Don River with Toronto's harbour to erect a wind-powered flour mill, eastern Toronto's first industry. He was later joined by his brother-in-law, William Gooderham. It was common in pioneer Canada to use second-grade grain from grist-mill operations to produce whiskey. And the Gooderham and Worts mill did just that.

In the 1850s both the Great Western Railway and Grand Trunk Railway completed their lines into Toronto, and the waterfront boomed with industry. In 1859, Gooderham and Worts added a magnificent limestone distillery, the beginning of an expansion phase that lasted until 1890. By 1861 the company was producing 6,000 gallons of whiskey a day, and by 1870 it was responsible for one third of Canada's rye whiskey production. Extensive sections of the waterfront were filled in and the Don River was straightened, and soon the

The Gooderham and Worts industrial complex, a candidate for World Heritage designation.

plant was nowhere near the lake. But with a railway siding beside the distillery, water transport was no longer needed.

In 1928 the firm merged with Hiram Walker of Windsor, and the Gooderham and Worts facility became a secondary production plant. In 1986 it was purchased by Allied Lyons of England. Four years later it was declared obsolete and closed. A century and a half of liquor production had ended.

Because it had been relegated to a lesser role in its later years, the entire complex was little altered, and remained much as it had appeared in the 1890s. Its size and age make it one of Canada's most remarkable historic industrial complexes, earning it recognition as a National Historic Site.

Still, for fifteen years the site sat vacant, although popular for movie shoots. Its brick streets and authentic facades provided set

pieces for period movies such as *X-Men*, *The Hurricane* and the Academy Award-winning *Chicago*, as well as dozens of sketches in the television show *Kids in the Hall*. It is claimed that more than eight hundred movies and commercials have used the grounds for film sets.

In 2002, the entire complex was purchased by a group called Cityscape, which converted the two dozen buildings into a haven for artists and galleries, and in May of 2003, the "Distillery District" was formally opened. Various rooms, including the smoke house, the boiler house, the malting plant and the pure-spirits building, are now occupied by galleries, studios, bars and cafés. Where possible, early machinery has been left in place.

74

Tiny cottages with no roads, only sidewalks, make for an unusual landscape on Toronto's islands. Many island cottages enjoy a harbourside view of Toronto's skyline.

COTTAGE COUNTRY SOUTH
The Toronto Island Community

O N THE EAST end of the island archipelago known collectively as the Toronto Islands are cottages unlike any that are found elsewhere in Ontario. In fact, they are no longer real "cottages" but have become permanent homes.

The island chain was at one time a sandy spit of land jutting into the lake. In 1858 a vicious storm sent waves hurtling across the narrow isthmus, so strong that they opened a new channel, turning the sand spit into a chain of islands.

Several amusement parks sprang up along the lake at spots both east and west of the industrial core, including Hanlan's Point on the Toronto Islands. Hotels, dance halls and rides drew Torontonians to the island haven. There was for a time a baseball stadium located where today's island airport is situated.

At the same time on Ward's Island, down at the east end of the chain, a campground appeared. Campers originally paid $10 for the season to pitch their tents. But the demand grew to such an extent that the government laid out "streets" and designated lots for each tent. As time went by, floors were added, as were kitchens and then porches. Finally permanent buildings replaced the tents. Then in 1953, the newly amalgamated Metropolitan Toronto government assumed ownership of the island and set about removing the buildings. But the government hadn't counted upon the tenacity of the cottage owners, who by now were occupying their dwellings year round.

Despite ongoing efforts by the Metro government to have them evicted, cottage owners were eventually granted 99-year leases. And so there they stay.

The island allows no cars; residents move about by foot or bicycle. The lots on which the buildings stand remain the size of a tent site. No roads run between them, simply sidewalks. More than 260 homes crowd the islands, a smaller number of them on nearby Algonquin Island. The styles and methods of decorating are eclectic, with statuary, sculptures and vines all adorning the tiny homes. Islanders work, shop and play for the most part on the mainland, connected by frequent ferry service.

Beyond Ward's Island lie luxurious yacht clubs and the concrete steps and foundations of those homes that were removed earlier on. Other historic structures include the 1809 Gibraltar Point lighthouse, said to be haunted by its first keeper; a church rectory that now serves as a delightful restaurant; the lovely white, wooden St. Andrews-by-the-Lake Anglican Church; and the historic airport terminal building.

75

Shoppers and tourists can learn Midland's history from its giant outdoor murals.

MIDLAND'S GIANT OUTDOOR ART GALLERY

THEY SAVED A B.C. town from becoming a ghost town, and now they have turned the faltering port of Midland into a tourist attraction. They are giant outdoor murals.

During the 1970s, the sawmill town of Chemainus, on Vancouver Island, faced the loss of its sole industry. Disaster seemed imminent. To cushion the blow, the town hired leading muralists to turn their central streets into an outdoor art gallery. The paintings, which depict scenes from local history and culture, proved successful beyond the residents' grandest hopes, and today the little town draws more tourists than any other Island attraction outside Victoria.

The idea was quickly copied by towns in Ontario that were facing similar downturns. Beginning in the 1950s, the Georgian Bay port of Midland began to lose its industries. The key shipyards closed, followed by the grain elevators and finally, in the 1980s, the Canadian National removed its line into the town.

In 1991, the town commissioned renowned artist Fred Lenz to paint a series of murals throughout the downtown area. As the murals gained in popularity, the town hired other artists, including Dan Sawatsky, who had created some of Chemainus' finer works. Today more than thirty murals look out over Midland's downtown core.

Most of the murals lie along King

Street—the main drag—between Elizabeth and the waterfront. They portray Midland's early history, with images of schooners, mills and stores. A three-panel mural shows a steam engine puffing into the town's railway station, while another depicts wildlife at the nearby Wye Marsh.

The grandest mural, however, decorates the side of the former Ogilvie grain elevator that looms above the water, across the harbour from the foot of the main street. Here the viewer can admire Fred Lenz's rendering of an early Jesuit missionary meeting members of the Huron tribe.

While working on the mural, Lenz suffered a heat attack and died. Family and friends took up his brushes and finished the work.

While several other towns across Ontario have tried to emulate Midland's success, the tiny port's murals remain one of Ontario's finest outdoor art galleries.

THE CHELTENHAM BADLANDS

Ontario's Painted Desert

MANY WESTWARD-BOUND Ontarians make Drumheller, Alberta, one of their must-sees. For here, thousands of years of water and wind erosion have worn through layers of shale to create a landscape of barren hills and gullies punctuated by remnant pillars known as "hoodoos." While the desert-like terrain spurned farmers and ranchers, it did expose coal seams and a rich source of dinosaur bones.

But drylands are expected in the west. They are less so in lush, forested Ontario. Known as Medina shale, a deposit of red-and-green sediment appears throughout the Niagara Escarpment area, but nowhere is it so dramatically exposed as in a 37-hectare hillside north of the village of Cheltenham. Here, the shale has been sculpted into a dramatic landscape of smooth ridges and gullies, totally bereft of vegetation.

The age of the ancient seabed is estimated at 450 million years, not a period of dinosaur activity. And unlike in Alberta, the feature here is not entirely natural. Until the settlers arrived, the deposit lay beneath a forest and soil cover. But once the settlers cleared the land and began to graze their cattle, erosion of the hillside exposed the colourful layers. So hard was the exposed material that grasses and shrubs were unable to take hold. However, like those in Alberta, Ontario's badlands revealed an economic resource, the ingredients for brickmaking, that brought a boom to the area.

The deposit also gave rise to a number of brickmaking villages in the area, such as Terra Cotta and the Cheltenham brickyards. When the brickmaking ceased, the villages dwindled. Terra Cotta remains a residential community, but the Cheltenham site now contains only the gaunt skeletal shells of the old kilns.

Located beside Old Baseline Road between Highway 10 and Mississauga Road, the ridges and gullies, with their colourful layers, have long been a local landmark — and a destination for many a geography class. The dramatic landscape has also attracted film location scouts seeking unusual topography for their sets. The site was acquired by the Ontario government in 1999 and transferred to the Ontario Heritage Foundation. It is managed by the Bruce Trail Association as part of its trail system.

76

An unexpected site on Ontario's otherwise green landscape
are these badlands near Cheltenham.

77

Neglected and forgotten Niagara-on-the-Lake's Fort Mississauga
now endures a barrage of golf balls from the course on which it sits.

FORT MISSISSAUGA
The Forgotten Fort

ROUND AND HARD, the missiles speed through the air, crashing against the walls of the ancient fort. Bricks and mortar splatter into the air and fall to the ground.

Niagara-on-the-Lake's Fort Mississauga is being assaulted, not by enemy batteries, but rather by errant golfers on the golf course that now surrounds it. The fort was hurriedly built in 1814 on the site of an earlier Seneca fishing village from the rubble of an old lighthouse to stave off a repeat of an earlier American attack.

The fort sustained a garrison only until 1826. It was re-manned in 1837 during the Upper Canada rebellion of that year, and again during the American Civil War and the Fenian troubles. Later, it was used as a training camp during the various wars of the twentieth century. For all that, Fort Mississauga never had a hostile shot fired at it.

Although small, it remains the only example of a star-shaped military earthwork in Canada. In addition to the brick tower and the tunnel to the lake that you see today, the fort originally consisted of a barracks, guardroom and cells as well.

In 1976 when Parks Canada, which had so masterfully restored the much larger Fort George a short distance away, indicated its intention to restore Fort Mississauga, the golfers rebelled and won the day. Although Parks Canada has retained ownership and has stabilized the walls, they have left the fort a ruin. And that is what makes the fort unusual and enhances its appeal.

It is accessible along a trail from the corner of Front and Simcoe streets in the historic heart of the town. The town, of course, has much to offer the history lover, for it has retained its nineteenth-century ambience though careful preservation and restoration of many of its early buildings. The restored Fort George is worth a visit, as is the Niagara Apothecary, run by the Ontario College of Pharmacy as a Confederation-era drugstore. The town is best noted for its annual Shaw Festival, an event that brings theatre lovers to share the history of this picturesque Lake Ontario town.

TEMPLE OF LIGHT 78
The Sharon Temple

GROUPS LIKE THE Quakers and the Shakers, the Mormons and the Mennonites, all originated with "visionaries" who led a group of dedicated followers away from the mainstream denominations. While all were present in pioneer Ontario, none left so prominent a landmark as did David Willson and his Children of Peace.

In 1801, Willson, a Quaker, migrated from New York to the Newmarket area of Upper Canada, where his Society of Friends brethren (as the Quakers were called) were particularly active. However, Willson grew impatient with the local leadership and decided to have a vision of his own. His vision was to restore his form of Christianity to its Judaic roots.

In 1825, Willson and his Children of Peace began construction of an elaborate and highly symbolic temple. When finished, the three-storey structure resembled a windowed wedding cake and totally dominated the landscape of simple pioneer buildings. Centre doors on each side symbolized the equal acceptance of people from all directions, while the square shape, it is said, meant the group dealt "squarely" with everyone. Inside, twelve pillars represented the twelve apostles.

Then, as now, religious leaders displayed a strong sense of self. Inside the temple Willson placed a decorative altar that was partially enclosed, while on the grounds outside the temple he built his small but equally ornate personal study. The Children of Peace celebrated two festivals, Willson's own birthday, dubbed the "Feast of the Passover," and the fall "Feast of Illumination," when the Children placed 116 candles in their temple windows.

Willson's death in 1866 signalled the downfall of the Children of Peace. By 1890 they were extinct, and the temple vacant. But in 1919, a far-sighted York Pioneer and Historical Society acquired the temple and converted it into a museum.

And so it remains today. On the outskirts of Sharon, now a Toronto bedroom community, visitors may view the temple, little changed in a century and a half. Although other pioneer buildings, including an 1852 township hall, have been moved onto the grounds, the story of David Willson and his Children of Peace brings to life a small but highly unusual chapter of our pioneer past. The stunning temple is on Leslie Street in Newmarket, a short distance north of Green Lane.

One of the most unusual churches ever constructed in Ontario is Sharon Temple, built by the equally unusual Quaker sect known as the Children of Peace.

THE DUTCH CHAPEL 79
The Pillars of the Scarborough Bluffs

A MONG SOUTHERN ONTARIO'S more unusual natural features are the Scarborough Bluffs. Not only do the craggy 20-kilometre-long forms loom up to 100 metres over Lake Ontario between the eastern end of the Beaches and the Rouge River, but their fractured and ever-eroding face reveals to scientists and laymen alike the mysteries of central Ontario's prehistoric past.

Unlike the tiny trickle that is today's Don River, Toronto was once the site of a mighty pre-glacial torrent, greater than the St. Lawrence. Here, more than seventy thousand years ago, these rushing waters poured into a great lake and there deposited an extensive delta. Then the ice age, with glaciers often more than 2 kilometres thick, deposited more boulder clay on top of the delta.

As the last ice sheets melted away twelve thousand years ago, and the lakes behind them drained, the delta stood like a mighty mesa above what was then a barren landscape. Wind, water and frost then began to eat away at its southern face. The alternating layers of soft, pure sand and rock-hard clay created oddly shaped pinnacles and buttresses. So closely did the rugged shoreline resemble her beloved Yorkshire homeland, that the wife of Upper Canada's first governor, John Graves Simcoe, named them the Scarborough Bluffs.

In a quiet gully at the foot of Scarborough's Midland Avenue, erosion has created a series of buttresses somewhat like the architecture found in medieval European chapels, and geologists have named the area the Dutch Chapel.

The constant and unpredictable erosion has forced the removal of many homes, which had been built too close to the brink.

Today, most visit "the Bluffs," as they are called locally, to picnic in the popular Bluffers Park located at the foot of Brimley Road. Here are beaches, restaurants, yachts, houseboats and unsightly marinas. But the centre of attraction remains the towering cliff face, within which is a story that is seventy thousand years old.

The Dutch Chapel, Scarborough Bluffs.

TORONTO ISLAND'S HAUNTED LIGHTHOUSE
80

O NTARIO'S OLDEST STANDING lighthouse is haunted, some say, by the ghost of its first keeper. Constructed of huge limestone blocks, the hexagonal 20-metre structure was built in 1808 at Gibraltar Point, on what is now the Toronto Island archipelago, before there was a Toronto, and even before there were islands. (In 1834 the Town of York became the City of Toronto. The islands were actually a peninsula until 1858, when a vicious storm hurled waves across its narrow, sandy neck, severing it from the mainland.)

When the lighthouse was completed, John Paul Radan Muller was appointed its keeper and he moved into a small log cabin beside it. In April 1813, he watched helplessly as Colonel Pearce guided fourteen American ships past the lighthouse and landed the troops that would capture York, in one of the few American victories of the War of 1812.

Just two years later, Radan Muller disappeared in circumstances that the *York Gazette* described as "moral proof of having been murdered." It would later add that there was "no conviction of the supposed murder." Was he murdered by drunken companions? Did he renege on a bootlegging operation then being run from the military base?

Although the former whale-oil lamp has been replaced by modern navigational aids, the lighthouse remains virtually unaltered. Yet, around it, an entire chapter in Toronto's history has started and finished. By the 1920s, the islands had become a popular recreational complex of amusement parks, hotels and private cottages. It was here in the island baseball stadium that baseball legend Babe Ruth hit his first professional home run into the waters of the lake.

Today, Gibraltar Point is a passive recreational area where trees, grass and trails have replaced the buildings of a bygone day. And the changes are all carefully watched over by the lighthouse and its keeper.

The old stone lighthouse on Toronto Island's Gibraltar Point is said to be haunted by its first keeper.

A Horse Palace
The Casa Loma Stables

CASA LOMA DOMINATES Toronto's brochures, has felt the footsteps of millions of tourists, and has been the location of dozens of movie shoots. Toronto's best-known landmark is also its only castle. Less well known are the incredible Casa Loma stables. In fact, these elegant barns were finished a full four years before construction on the Casa even started. With their castle-like towers and turrets, they are considered the most lavish stables on the continent.

The castle's owner and builder was Sir Henry Pellatt. A multimillionaire, Pellatt earned his riches by investing in land along the newly built Canadian Pacific Railway to the west. He used those earnings to build Canada's first hydro generating station at Niagara Falls.

But he also loved the military and castles, and in 1905 he purchased twenty residential lots on top of the Davenport Escarpment. He then hired architect Edward James Lennox, designer of the city's most prominent buildings (including the old city hall), to design his castle. By 1914, the dream castle was complete on the outside. Huge cost overruns, however, prevented him from finishing the interior. After ten years, his wife's illness and financial ruin forced him to flee the castle.

Interestingly, the lesser-known stables more truly reflect the lifestyle and tastes of this mysterious man. Described as the most lavish anywhere on the continent, the buildings were completed in 1906. Inside, the stalls are of mahogany, with the horses' names spelled out in gold lettering above each. The floors were covered in Spanish tiles, laid in a herringbone pattern so that horses would not slip. Pellatt's favourite horse, named Prince, was even outfitted with a set of false teeth. The entrance is framed in white stone to contrast with the red brick of the building.

Adjoining the stables, the carriage house boasts a room larger even than the castle's main hall. Here, Pellatt stored his magnificent collection of carriages and Toronto's first electric car. The stables and carriage room are connected to the castle by a 150-metre-long tunnel.

Casa Loma and its stables are located on Spadina Road, north of Davenport Road.

Casa Loma's stable was as grand as the "castle" itself.

The Yorkville Rock sparked controversy when it was moved
from Gravenhurst to Toronto.

THE YORKVILLE ROCK

THE ROCK IS more than a billion years old, weighs 650 tonnes and cost $300,000, yet it contains no precious metals or minerals. Plunked right in the middle of Toronto's priciest shopping district, it is known, somewhat derogatorily, as the "Yorkville Rock."

In 1966, Toronto's new east-west subway slashed through the hippy haven known as Yorkville Village, a collection of coffee houses tucked into a row of nineteenth-century homes. Although the little neighbourhood evolved into an ever-pricier shopping area, the subway route had left a no-man's land on which nothing heavy could be built. For years the strip of land remained an unsightly parking lot.

Finally, in 1991 the City of Toronto and the local business association hired architect Olesand Worland to create a park to befit both the context and the history of the area. In just one city block, his park would display the ecological variety of the entire province. While the trees and the flowers presented no problem, Toronto offered nothing that resembled Ontario's most extensive landscape element, the Canadian Shield, whose hard, rounded rocks are the oldest on Earth. The nearest outcrops were over 150 kilometres away.

The solution he proposed was to move a granite outcrop from Gravenhurst to Toronto, a procedure that would cost more than a quarter of a million dollars. The first reaction was ridicule and outrage; however, the park not only proceeded, but opened in 1994 to widespread acclaim from architects and users alike. In one city block the visitor can travel from a garden with bluebells and trilliums to an alder grove, a wetland and a herb garden. At the end of the provincial mini-tour, the visitor has lunch or reads a book on top of a billion-year-old rock. The park stretches along the south side of Cumberland Avenue, between Avenue Road and Bellair Street.

Although equally acclaimed, the award-winning Cloud Gardens, in the heart of Toronto's financial district, has fared less well. In contrast to the much-visited Yorkville park, Cloud Gardens is little more than a haven for the homeless and a gathering place for downtown bike couriers.

Designed by Margaret Priest, the small lot on Temperance Street between Yonge and Bay contains urban woodland, waterfalls and an observation platform. Situated over the entrance to a parking garage is a glass-enclosed "Cloud Forest" conservatory, with its re-creation of a tropical rain forest. Surrounded by the glass towers of the Bay Street brokers, this intriguing urban park won a Governor-General's Medal for Architecture in 1994 and a merit award from the Canadian Society of Landscape Architects the next year.

PERFECT PURIFICATION
The Elevated Wetlands of the Don Valley

THE ELEVATED WETLANDS of the Don Valley have drivers on the busy Don Valley Parkway blinking in disbelief. At the Don Mills Road exit are a half-dozen massive plant pots. To some, they may look more like giant topless teapots; to others, grotesque mastodons performing some form of daisy chain. They are in fact an innovative system of purifying the waters of the Don River using only plastic.

In 1995, the Canadian Plastics Industry Association hired artist Noel Harding to create a public work of art that would help illustrate the artistic potential of that industrial material. Harding, a sculptor who pushes the limits of both sculpture and material, is well known for his Potato Eaters sculpture. This series of metal structures is 12 to 25 metres high, each containing a living tree, and helped earn him international attention at the Atlanta Olympics.

Inside the giant pots in the Don Valley are various types of plastic, all shredded, including bottles, resins, auto fluff and geo textiles. A cluster of solar panels pumps water from the Don River into the highest of the pots. Here, plants, shrubs and trees draw the pollutants and toxins from the water and return it perfectly pure. More than seventy different industries helped sponsor the unusual project, including fifty plastics industries. The sculptures, which measure between 8 and 15 metres high, were created between 1997 and 1998 and developed from a prototype developed at the University of Lethbridge.

Harding's is not the only effort to clean up the river. A short distance downstream, the Friends of the Don won a $100,000 grant from the Ontario government to excavate a century and a half of industrial residue from the flood plain. They replaced the landfill with a natural wetland ecosystem which, like the elevated wetlands, provides free water purification.

The strange sculptures can be seen up close from Taylor Creek Park on Don Mills Road, just north of the Don Valley Parkway. The marshland lies to the south of the Bloor Viaduct and can be accessed from the bike trail that follows the valley.

83

The Don Valley Parkway's elevated wetlands.

THE LAKE WITH NO WAVES
The Strange Story of Crawford Lake

THE CRAWFORD LAKE Conservation Area is a rare find. It sits atop the Niagara Escarpment with wonderful views and trails that wind through a hardwood forest. It also has a small lake, but this is a lake with no waves.

Geologists even have a special name for it, a meromectic lake, which means that, relative to its surface area, it is disproportionately deeper than most lakes, to the point that waves seldom occur and the bottom sediments remain undisturbed. In effect, it is ecologically like two lakes, one on top of the other. The lower levels are deprived of the oxygen that would normally come from the air above, thus preserving the material on the bottom.

Such preservation allows scientists to read this debris and determine with much more certainty what the area around it was like thousands of years ago. Lake Crawford is estimated to be at least fifteen thousand years old.

Among the layers of silt that cover the bottom, scientists uncovered evidence of early Huron habitation. This discovery sent archaeologists searching the area around the lake, where they uncovered the remains of a previously unknown Huron village. The village contained nine longhouses for a population of about 450, and dates from around AD 1430. Numerous other village sites were subsequently recorded in the surrounding hills and valleys.

Not only are the shape and morphology of the lake unusual, so too is its origin. Unlike other lakes, which form along existing rivers or in lowlands, this one occurred, some theorize, when a cave beneath the upper limestone layer suddenly collapsed. Water rushed in from underground streams, quickly filling the cavity. Another theory suggests that the lake fills an ancient post-glacial spillway.

In 1969 the land was sold to the Halton Region Conservation Authority, which laid out trails and re-created the Huron village, complete with palisade. So authentic is the habitation and the depiction of the lifestyles of its inhabitants that it has become a must-see for many school children from across Ontario

A 1.4-kilometre path leads to the lake from the gate, where interpretive signs explain its unusual origins and composition. A 7.2-kilometre trail leads further afield, through the dark woodlands, to a lookout point over the scenic Nassagaweya Canyon. The park is on the Guelph Line, a short distance south of Highway 401.

84

Crawford Lake is one of only two deep oxygen-deprived meromectic lakes in Ontario.

85

The subdivision's wide streets give the historic community a modern appearance.

Markham Heritage Estates

A Suburb of Last Resort

WHERE DO CENTURY-OLD farmhouses go when urban sprawl engulfs the cornfields? Sadly, most fall beneath the wrecker's ball to be replaced by an endless sea of look-alike new homes. But in the heritage-conscious community of Markham, historic houses are given a new lease on life.

Markham, a fast-growing area of big-box stores, endless malls and gridlocked traffic, sits on the northeastern fringe of the Greater Toronto Area. But despite this unchecked growth, Markham retains much of its built heritage.

That heritage dates back to the 1790s, when William Berczy led a group of colonizers from the United States to the headwaters of the Rouge and Don rivers. In the years that followed, farm villages and mill towns appeared across the landscape. One of the most successful was Markham. In 1871, the Toronto and Nipissing Railway built a station a short distance north of Markham's mills, and the community boomed.

And thanks to Markham's citizens and politicians, much of that heritage has been retained. The historic main street, like that in the smaller village of Unionville a few kilometres west, has been historically refurbished, and new development must be compatible with the historic theme. North of the main street, the original station has been restored to its original appearance and reopened as a GO commuter station and community facility.

And then there are the Markham Heritage Estates. Faced with the loss of countless historic farmhouses and village homes to urban sprawl, the Town of Markham gave the houses a home. In 1996, Markham created, adjacent to its museum village, a plan of a subdivision, with thirty-eight lots, solely for the purpose of relocating threatened heritage houses. Under the plan, the Town of Markham sells the lots at less than market value to owners of heritage homes that are threatened with demolition. The amount saved on the price of the lot provides the owners with the incentive to relocate and restore the house in the new location.

Among the oldest of the relocated houses are the David Leek Houses built in 1840 and formerly located in the vanished village of Dollar, and the 1845 house built by Richard Lewis in the community of Gormley. For its heritage initiatives, Markham was awarded the coveted Prince of Wales Prize in 1999.

Markham Heritage Estates is located next to 16th Avenue, west of Highway 48.

86

Other than the monument, little remains of Camp X, the top-secret war facility where James Bond was born in the mind of author Ian Fleming.

James Bond and the Secret of Camp X

Cloak-and-dagger movies and spy thrillers like the James Bond books conjure images of stealth, danger and sultry temptresses. In reality, undercover work was humdrum. Most espionage work involved censoring mail, breaking codes and forging diplomatic documents. Canada's most secret Second World War spy-training facility was known simply as Camp X.

Located on a then-isolated Lake Ontario shoreline, midway between Oshawa and Whitby, Camp X was the responsibility of a man called "Intrepid." In real life he was William (later Sir William) Stephenson. Born in Winnipeg, the decorated First World War flying ace was put in charge of British counterespionage at the camp.

The camp consisted of two components. One was the Special Training School, or STS 103, focused on spy training. A second, even more secret activity, code-named Hydra, involved top-secret messages sent between the United States and Canada. So sensitive was the work that any outsiders who ventured near it were to be shot on sight.

After the war, Camp X continued as a government communications centre until 1969. Even then its wartime secrets remained locked away. Only after the buildings were demolished or removed were the secret activities at Camp X finally revealed.

While Stephenson became the subject of books (*A Man Called Intrepid*), another Camp X visitor went on to write them. Ian Fleming, a commander of British naval intelligence, used his spy training to create a fictional super spy named James Bond.

When the legends of Camp X finally became public, a park was opened on the site of the camp. Created in 1984, Intrepid Park features a large monument erected to commemorate those who worked there. On the base of the monument, photographs and text depict the story of the camp and its contribution to the Allied victory. From the monument, trails lead to an isolated beach on Lake Ontario, where camp artifacts that had been dumped into the lake wash ashore from time to time.

While most of the camp's buildings were demolished, some were removed to other sites. A former barracks is located at the Whitby Humane Society, on Thickson Road. Rare Camp X artifacts, formerly on display at Oshawa's Robert Stuart Museum, were auctioned off in 2011. However, many Camp X photos may be found at www.camp-x.com. No longer isolated, Camp X today is surrounded by industrial sprawl. The park and monument can be found on Boundary Road, on the Oshawa-Whitby border.

87

The faces of Old City Hall.

THE FEELING OF BEING WATCHED

Toronto's Old City Hall Gargoyles

Have you ever had the feeling that you're being watched? Stand in front of Toronto's Old City Hall and you are — by its gargoyles!

Old City Hall is a remarkable example of the Victorian Romanesque Revival architectural style. Completed in 1899, it was one of those grand municipal buildings typical of the period. With its tall clock tower dominating Bay Street, each nook and cranny — and there are many — of its sandstone exterior seems to offer a different architectural surprise, especially the gargoyles. While such grotesque faces were common on medieval buildings, some of those on Old City Hall carried a special meaning.

City architect E. J. Lennox had staked much of his reputation on what he hoped would be his masterpiece. But when the Toronto city council of the day short-changed him, or so he thought, he decided to even the score. There, above the grand entrance, sits E. J. Lennox's revenge: the gargoyles are the distorted faces of the councillors themselves. In a final act of defiance, Lennox added, contrary to instructions, his own name and a caricature said to resemble himself. Old City Hall is festooned with dozens of the more traditional gargoyles — grotesque animal-like faces. But the faces of the Toronto council of the day will live on in a way none had likely intended.

Much of Victorian Toronto has vanished. Fine old buildings of stone or brick have fallen victim to insensitive redevelopment, and to builders whose bottom line doesn't include a respect for heritage. Even Old City Hall itself was threatened when the Eaton Centre was proposed. But citizen outrage saved the building, which today functions as a court. And so, amid modern glass and concrete towers, the gargoyles of Toronto's Old City Hall still keep watch.

ORANGEVILLE'S TREE SPIRITS

88

MANY RELIGIONS AFFIRM that following death, a person's spirit lives on, perhaps even reincarnated as another being. Few, however, would suggest that the same holds true for trees — that is, until they go to Orangeville.

Orangeville began life as a mill town around 1829 when John Corbit arrived and found a small millstream engulfed by towering pine trees and wide, shady maples. Orange Lawrence came on the scene in 1844 and opened the post office, naming the town after himself.

The community remained a small mill village until two railway lines converged on the site. As the main street grew into an avenue of stately brick stores and an elegant town hall, maple trees were planted along the streets in the residential sections of town. In the last few decades, Orangeville's growth has accelerated, turning it into a booming bedroom community for cities like Toronto and Mississauga.

Those stately maples, however, have not been so lucky. Pollution from passing trucks and simple old age have brought them to the end of their years. Most communities would cut such trees off at the base, yank out the roots and plant some newer, more exotic species that would be lucky to survive the salt of the winter. But not so in Orangeville.

The idea was Mayor Drew Brown's. While visiting Truro, Nova Scotia, Brown noticed that tree trunks were often carved into historical figures. He returned to his hometown and planted the notion that the town's doomed maples trees could enjoy, if not prolonged life, at least an "afterlife."

In 2002, the carvers began. The trees were cut down to 3 or 4 metres in height and seventeen renowned carvers, including Colin Partridge, Jim Menken, Walter vanderWindt and Peter Mogensen, began turning the lifeless trunks into eagles, Indians, dancers, fiddlers, bears, historic figures and tree spirits — this last the main subject of carver Colin Partridge. Almost three dozen carvings now line the streets of Orangeville.

Most line the north side of Broadway, the main street, west of downtown. Another cluster lines First Street north of Broadway. The remainder are scattered throughout the town. Much like the main street murals of Midland, Ontario, and Chemainus, British Columbia, the dead trees of Orangeville have helped turn the town into one of Ontario's more unusual tourist attractions.

Add to that Orangeville's regular theatre productions and the scenic tour train, and the dead here have truly gained new life.

A Tree Spirit entitled "The Indian" was carved by Jeff Waters.

89

Shanty Bay's Anglican church is perhaps North America's only example of a "mud church."

THE MUD CHURCH OF SHANTY BAY

CANADIANS HAVE LONG looked to nature for building material. Bark and skins were used by Aboriginal inhabitants. The first shanties of the European arrivals were hastily erected from logs, while prairie pioneers were noted for their early sod huts. And where stones were plentiful they were used for homes, churches and schools.

While adobe brick was commonly used in the southwestern U.S., it was rarely employed in Canada, owing largely to its vulnerability to rain. But one ingredient was so rarely used that only one building of any significance in Canada is known to have used it, and that ingredient is mud.

Common in medieval Europe, it is also known as cob, or "rammed earth" construction, and consists of a mixture of clay, sand and straw. The three ingredients are mixed into a dough-like substance and pressed, or rammed, into a wall mould. It is then covered with plaster or wood. The only building of such size to be made of the mud, some say in all of North America, is St. Thomas Anglican Church in a hamlet on Lake Simcoe named Shanty Bay.

The church was started in 1837 on land donated by the founder of the Shanty Bay settlement, Colonel Edward O'Brien. The mud walls, 1 metre thick, were laid on a stone foundation. Wood was hand hewn from local supplies of pine, ash and cedar — the axe marks remain visible to this day. The original square pews are still used as well.

Despite the unusual construction technique, you wouldn't know it to look at it. With its stucco finish, it resembles many a church of the era, solid and Gothic, with a handsome steeple. In only a few sections of the lower wall is the mud exposed.

The church, which remains in full use, lies south of Ridge Road in the centre of the village, about 8 kilometres east of Barrie. The name of the village itself dates to the 1830s as well, when the community was a jumping-off point for Black settlers en route to farm lots north of the lake. Their settlement has also left its religious imprint in the Oro African Church, built in 1848 and located on the Old Barrie Road at the east end of the village of Edgar, about 10 kilometres from Shanty Bay.

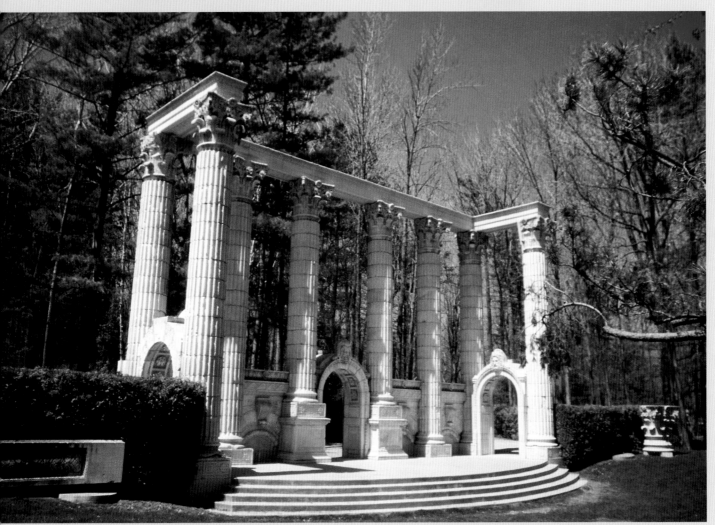

90

The rescued remains of Toronto's demolished buildings decorate the Guild Inn's gardens.

Top: Terracotta turrets from the Produce Exchange Building have become the rear gates to the Garden of Ruins.

THE GUILD INN'S GARDEN OF RUINS

IN 1914, GENERAL Harold C. Bickford built a country home on the Scarborough Bluffs. He called his two-and-a-half-storey house Ranelagh Park. In 1932, Rosa and Spencer Clark bought the home with its 162 hectares and established the Guild of All Arts. Here the Clarks hoped to help artists survive the difficult Depression years by giving them a home where they could practise their crafts. As the guild expanded, a dining room and more guest rooms were added, turning the facility into a popular resort under a new name — the Guild Inn.

After 1947, the couple became alarmed at the rate at which Toronto's many heritage buildings were being demolished. To help preserve part of this vanishing heritage, they began to acquire remnants of these elegant structures. And so began the garden of ruins.

In the garden, which stretches between the inn and the lake, lurk the vestiges of banks, homes, schools and industrial buildings: a white marble facade from the Imperial Bank of Canada (1875); a cornerstone and cornice from the Imperial Oil Company building; white terracotta Ionic capitals from the University of Toronto's Faculty of Medicine building; bas-relief panels from the Bank of Montreal buildings at King and Bay, from the Toronto Globe and Mail building (1938) and from the Toronto Star building (1929); as well as stone carvings and keystones from the O'Keefe Brewery (1840), the Ontario Bank (1868), and the Toronto General Post Office (1873).

Pillars and columns survive from the 1895 Temple Building, the 1915 Registry of Deeds and Lands Titles building and the 1913 Bank of Nova Scotia building. But the most photographed relic is the Greek Theatre built in 1981 from eight of the original twenty-one Corinthian capitals and columns belonging to the Bank of Toronto. The bank was built in 1912 and demolished in 1966.

In all, nearly sixty ruins and remnants lie scattered throughout a formal garden setting. In 1978, the gardens were transferred to the Toronto and Region Conservation Authority, while the inn, with a modern hotel tower attached, continued to provide meals and accommodation. The garden of ruins is now part of Toronto's system of attractive parks and remains a popular setting for wedding photography, providing a unique opportunity to witness part of Toronto's lost heritage. The Guild Inn is located on the Guildwood Parkway, south of Kingston Road.

Tiny Town

Toronto's Smallest Houses

91

Toronto's little nooks and crannies hide many surprises. While its older and architecturally more splendid buildings are widely known, smaller and simpler structures are often even more interesting because their odds of surviving demolition or alteration are comparatively slim. That's the case with Cabbagetown's tiny Wellesley Cottages, located just north of Wellesley Street at Sackville.

During the 1870s and '80s, Ontario's railway boom years, labourers' cottages, as they were called, were hastily built to house the influx of workers. Between then and the 1890s, thousands were constructed in working-class neighbourhoods all across Toronto. The Wellesley Cottages were built around 1886–87.

Constructed of wood, usually with no foundations, these tiny one-and-a-half-storey cabins all boasted a centre plan, and many had a trademark gable over the front door. The style earned its designers an architectural award for workmen's cottage design at the Crystal Palace Exhibit in England in 1851.

Over the years, demands for bigger and safer housing meant the end of a housing era in Toronto and the gradual disappearance of these simple abodes. Throughout the city only a few isolated examples survive, and the Wellesley Cottages are a remarkable row of seven. They are located not on a main residential street, but on a narrow lane behind the backyards of the principal row of houses. After being used for a time as low-cost rental units, they were sold to a developer who upgraded them.

Much of Old Cabbagetown is equally interesting. A stroll along Wellesley, Sumach (Cabbagetown's old-timers pronounce it "shoo-mack"), Spruce and Winchester streets reveals a residential neighbourhood of eclectic houses that date to the days when the area's low-income residents planted cabbages in their front yards, giving the community its unusual name. In this area you will also find the former Riverdale Zoo, now an animal farm for children.

For many years a 2.5-metre-wide house on Shuter Street, now enlarged, was considered Toronto's narrowest. However, an even narrower dwelling on Day Street in Toronto's west end now claims that title, being wedged between two larger two-storey homes.

Farther west of Shuter, another row of tiny nineteenth-century homes lines a narrow lane a block west of McCaul Street and a short distance north of Queen Street.

Toronto's tiniest house is dwarfed between two regular-sized homes in Toronto's west end.

The Last of the Water Mills

The Tyrone Mill

Within the sprawling Greater Toronto Area, there remains a tranquil oasis where visitors can return to simpler pleasures of pioneer Ontario. That retreat, one of the last commercially operated water-powered mills in the province, is found in the historic village of Tyrone.

As pioneer settlers pushed inland from Lake Ontario, James McFeeters built a flour mill on the waters of Bowmanville Creek, about 18 kilometres north of Bowmanville. It became the main industry in the growing little community. In 1908, with most of Canada's wheat-growing having moved west, then owner Thomas Goodman converted the building to a feed mill to provide feed for the growing dairy cattle industry.

But even that operation began to flag, bringing in less than $50 a year by the 1970s. At this point, most mills would have either burned or been converted to a restaurant. But Bob Shafer, a relocated American, had other plans. And that was to continue operating it as a mill, and not just any mill. It would be one that continued to use water. At first, he focused on custom cutting logs provided by local farmers. However, after locating a compatible turbine, he restored the mill's original role to that of grinding grain.

Today, the Tyrone mill has become a popular day trip destination for families and history lovers who wish to flee the maddening world of ceaseless traffic and the tedium of urban sprawl. The mill offers not just its own grain, but also fresh apple cider (in season) and its specialty, hot and tender freshly baked doughnuts.

Visitors may also climb the wooden steps to the second floor to view the woodworking room, where a system of pulleys is also run by water power. At the rear of the mill, a small lookout over the millpond may reveal ducks, geese and, possibly, a pair of swans.

Meanwhile, Tyrone's main street offers up other vestiges of Ontario's pioneer days, including an early schoolhouse, churches and a stone blacksmith shop.

92

The Tyrone mill near Bowmanville may be Ontario's
last commercially operated water-powered mill.

93

This structure housed the more senior German POWs.

Top: When prisoners tried to tunnel out of Bowmanville's POW Camp 30, the dirt they stored in the roof of the structure brought down the ceiling and foiled the attempt.

CAMP 30 AND THE BATTLE OF BOWMANVILLE

WITHIN THE GREATER Toronto Area there remains the only surviving intact World War Two prisoner of war camp in any of the former Allied countries.

In 1925 the property opened as a boys' training school. At the onset of World War Two, facilities were needed to house captured prisoners of war. Winston Churchill asked Canada to house the highest-ranking German officers. He wanted them kept as far as possible from the front, lest they escape and rejoin their units.

And so it was that, in November 1941, the three hundred boys were moved out and eight hundred high-ranking German officers, including generals, were escorted in. Because of the rules that governed captured soldiers, the prisoners were allowed to keep their uniforms and their ranks. Within the camp, prisoners did their own cooking, used the recreational facilities, formed a theatre group and orchestra, and even were allowed off the property to tend their own farm. While most of the eight hundred POWs were crammed into dorms designed for three hundred boys, the highest-ranking generals enjoyed the exclusive use of what had been built as a hospital for the juveniles. The most noted of the generals was von Ravenstein, who had served under Rommel on the African front.

As occurred in most POW camps, escapes were attempted. In one case, the POWs managed to complete a network of elaborate tunnels, only to have the ceiling, where they stored the dirt, collapse under the weight and foil the attempt. One escapee, a lieutenant Hayda, did manage to get as far as the Bay of Chaleur, where a German submarine lay in wait—as did the Canadian military, who marched the unfortunate Hayda back to Bowmanville.

Then in October 1942 came the "Battle of Bowmanville." On learning that the Allies had shackled a number of German POWs following the failed raid on Dieppe, the Germans retaliated by shackling Allied POWs. A furious Churchill sent orders to Bowmanville to similarly bind the high-ranking officers there. But the Germans would have none of it and barricaded themselves in the various buildings. Finally, after three days, the Canadian guards stormed through the upper windows, armed only with baseball bats. After a furious free-for-all, the POWs relented and agreed to the shackles. However, to maintain order and morale, the Canadians allowed the shackles to remain loosely applied and for the men to take turns wearing them.

Following the war, the site reverted to a training school—a role it played until 1979, when the property was sold to a religious order and subsequently left vacant.

94

The City of Barrie has carried out extensive repairs
to its historic Allandale Grand Trunk station.

Barrie's Allandale Train Station

Ontario's Grandest Wooden Station

CURVING ALONG THE western shore of Lake Simcoe's Kempenfeldt Bay stretches what is, simply put, Ontario's grandest wooden railway station.

Railway activity here dates to the building of Ontario's first railway line—the Ontario, Simcoe and Huron Railway, which opened in 1853. When the line was extended to Collingwood, it became the Northern Railway. Then the Northern and Pacific Junction Railway was extended from Allandale northward to Callander, Allandale became a bustling railway junction—so bustling, in fact, that in 1905 the new owners, the Grand Trunk Railway, decided that a new station was needed.

The elegant new station offered a rounded waiting room at the south, from which passengers could enjoy views of the scenic lake. Attached to the waiting room was one of the GTR's finest dining rooms, with twinned pillars that led to a grand hall where uniformed wait staff could attend to as many as fifty patrons. Attached to the grand hall was a brick structure that housed offices for railway staff.

In the 1950s the CNR closed the yards, moving staff to Capreol while the fine restaurant became a soda bar. In the 1980s, the waiting room was closed and passengers relegated to a small shelter.

Passenger trains such as VIA Rail's Canadian and the ONR's Northlander continued to use the station until the 1990s, when the CNR removed the tracks between Barrie and Orillia. Following its designation as a heritage station by the federal government, the station was briefly occupied by a local radio station.

In 2011, the City of Barrie acquired the property and began restoration work. With the exterior complete, work was halted by a certificate of pending litigation brought by a developer, later removed by the courts. In late 2013, the city restarted plans to partner with private concerns and conclude restoration.

Nearby Station Park, which contains the foundation of the old turntable and the former mechanical shop for the divisional yards, is now a tourist office and event venue.

95

Dutch-style homes in the Holland Marsh show Ansnorvelt's Dutch heritage.

ANSNORVELT
A Touch of Holland in the Holland Marsh

WHEN THE VAST bog known as the Holland Marsh was drained in 1925, a number of Dutch families took up farms. They were led by John Snor, head of the Netherlands Immigration Foundation in Hamilton. In the 1930s, concerned because unemployed Dutch immigrants to Canada faced deportation back to Holland, he assembled funding from the federal, provincial and Dutch governments to move them to a new beginning in the Holland Marsh.

Here, along a stretch of Dufferin Street, he acquired a 125-acre town site where the nineteen families set about constructing a Dutch-style village consisting of identical Dutch-style houses.

In addition to the houses, the village consisted of a school, a Christian Reform church and Haddres Holland Marsh Groceteriers. Each house was built above the ground to reduce damage from flooding. The village itself was named An Snor Velt, meaning "on Snor's field," and many of the streets bore such Dutch names as Bernhardt, Juliana, Wilhelmina and Emma. At the corner of Dufferin and Emma streets, a commemorative plaque celebrates John Snor and the heritage of his namesake village.

Over the intervening years, many of the homes have been altered or replaced, but the little Dutch row still exhibits the architectural flavour of the Netherlands homeland. The community lies along Dufferin Street north of Highway 9, surrounded still by the vast black soils of the fertile marshland.

GRIMSBY PARK
Ontario's Chautauqua

SURPRISES OFTEN WAIT in unexpected places. One of those places lies only a few metres from the busy Queen Elizabeth Highway near Grimsby. Along a labyrinth of narrow lanes are a cluster of colourful cabins and cottages. A cairn in their midst announces that here was the 1859 beginning of a Methodist meeting ground, where John Bowslaugh donated a parcel of his land on the shore of Lake Ontario. People gathered from throughout the Niagara Peninsula to listen to lectures and enjoy the lakeside breezes.

Then in 1874, the grounds evolved into the Ontario Methodist Campground Company, which created fifty-five cottage lots and added a wharf and a pair of hotels, while the Great Western Railway placed a small station on its line to serve the park. In 1888, a large domed temple arose in the midst of the cottages. Many of the cabins boasted decorative fretwork and colourful wooden exteriors. The popularity of the grounds set the template for the development of a similar but much grander

institution in upper New York State. That institution was Chautauqua.

But by 1912, the campground company was bankrupt and sold the property for an amusement park with a carousel, miniature railway, roller coaster and shooting gallery. In 1916, Canada Steamship Lines bought the park and added it to its growing list of amusement grounds.

But time has taken its toll. Canada Steamship Lines dropped its park system in the 1950s, fires destroyed the hotels and many of the tiny cottages, and the temple was demolished. In 1939 the QEW opened its four limited-access lanes to through traffic, and tourists began to bypass the site en route to more colourful places like Niagara Falls.

Although the narrow lanes with names like Auditorium Circle and Temple Lane, lined with tiny colourful houses, are now part of Grimsby's urban area, they remain an unusual enclave that recalls an earlier, simpler era. Access is via Bartlett Avenue from the QEW.

Decorative cottages recall the early days of historic Grimsby Park when it was the prototype for Chautauqua.

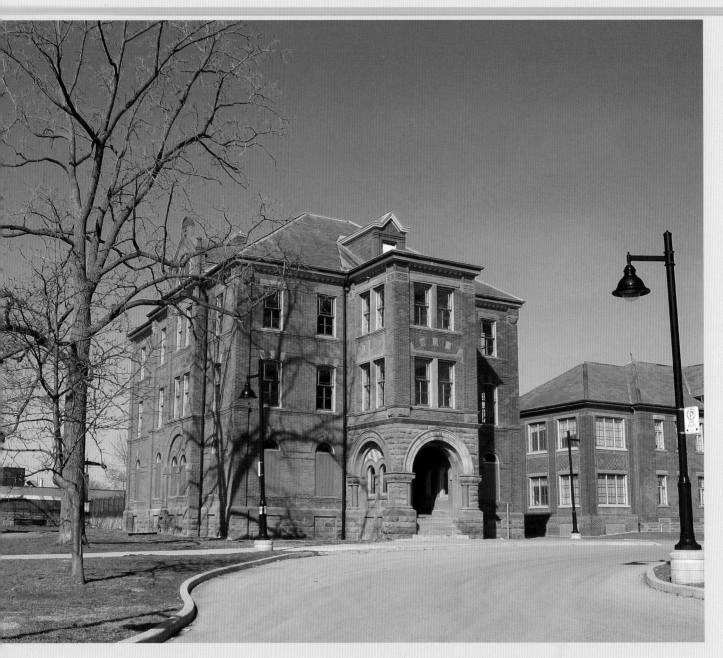

Now a Humber College campus, the buildings designed for the Mimico "lunatic asylum" offered early residents a more rural feel than did the previous hospital settings.

THE MIMICO ASYLUM

A New Lease on Life

THERE LIES AT the foot of Toronto's Kipling Avenue, where it meets Lakeshore Boulevard, a stunning set of brick and stone buildings. Now a part of the Humber College campus, it may be difficult to believe that they once housed a population of individuals who a century ago were categorized as "lunatics."

It all began with Dr. Daniel Clark, the superintendent of the then Queen Street Asylum for the insane in Toronto. He believed that institutionalization was of little benefit to its residents, and a village-style setting would aid in their rehabilitation. Along with provincial architect Kivas Tully and a landscape gardener named Samuel Matheson, Dr. Clark created such an environment on a 20-hectare parcel of land overlooking Lake Ontario in an area that at the time was farmland.

In 1889 the first residents moved to the new facility. The "village" consisted of a series of dormitories and an assembly hall. The asylum residents formed their own cricket team and farmed the land.

In 1911 it became the Mimico Hospital for the Insane. Soon the designation "insane" was removed, and it became the Ontario Hospital (New Toronto) and then the Lakeshore Psychiatric Hospital.

Then in 1979, badly overcrowded, the hospital closed its doors and became a popular location for the filming of movies, including *Police Academy*.

Because of the buildings' remarkable architecture and historic institutional role, the Ontario government designated them a provincial heritage district. In 1999 the assembly hall was renovated to become a community facility, and the remaining buildings redesigned to become a campus for Humber College.

98

The Welland Canal's three rare twin-flight locks ease massive ocean and Great Lakes vessels up and down the Niagara Escarpment.

Neptune's Staircase
The Welland Canal's Twin-Flight Locks

When the Erie Canal opened in 1826, it linked Lake Erie with the Atlantic Ocean at New York City. Meanwhile, the only all-Canadian route meant struggling up the rapids-strewn St. Lawrence River, and then overland to reach the upper lakes. It was quickly evident to William Hamilton Merritt that an all-Canadian canal was needed. By 1828, Merritt's canal opened between Port Dalhousie on Lake Ontario and Port Colborne on Lake Erie, and the all-Canadian alternative to the Erie Canal was bringing ships from Lake Ontario to Lake Erie.

But while construction between Lake Ontario and the Niagara Escarpment and from the top of the escarpment to Lake Erie was relatively straightforward, the problem lay with the 100-metre limestone cliff that formed the face of the escarpment. In the first version of the canal, of the forty locks, more than half were needed to climb the escarpment alone. Because of the step-like appearance of this series of locks, they earned the nickname "Neptune's Staircase."

Fifteen years later, a second canal replaced the narrow wooden locks of the first, reducing the number of locks from forty to twenty-seven. But again, a dozen locks were still needed to reach the lime-stone summit. Although the third canal, completed in 1887, succeeded in widening and deepening the locks, it failed to reduce the number required to climb the cliff. That did not occur until the fourth version of the canal opened to traffic in 1932, when a mere eight locks operated through the entire length — three at the cliff face itself.

As with the earlier structures, those three today are an engineering marvel. As the locks, 4, 5 and 6, feed into each other like a flight of stairs, they have also been twinned to allow vessels to pass through in each direction at the same time. Over a stretch of 1250 metres, the twin-flight locks lift or lower enormous ships by almost 43 metres, each operation requiring the draining and filling of more than 91 million litres of water. Yet incredibly, the entire process requires only ten minutes per lock.

The lock areas themselves are off limits, but a canal side road and trail allow visitors to pause and watch the passing of the ships as they inch into and out of the locks, often with less than a metre to spare on either side. Although the twin-flight locks are situated in the town of Thorold, a canal interpretative centre offers visitors a canal museum and platform from which to view the operations of lock 3 in the city of St. Catharines.

FATHER OF THE PEACE BRIDGE

Fort Erie's Mather Monument

As THE NIAGARA frontiers began to grow and boom on both sides of the churning Niagara River, among the only links between the two nations were the ferries that shuttled between Black Rock (near Buffalo) on the U.S. side, and Fort Erie on the Canadian. Finally in 1873, the great Canadian railway builder, Casimir Gzowski, designed a railway bridge to carry trains across the border. But that still left out pedestrians and vehicular traffic, although the auto age was still some years away.

Then in 1899, Alonzo Clark Mather, a Chicago inventor whose inventions had included a humanely designed railway car for transporting cattle and horses, saw the need for a bridge that not only would allow both rail and road traffic, but would also harness the power from the swift currents of the Niagara River sweeping below it. While railways would travel the central section, and pedestrians and wagon would use outer lanes, beneath the structure a series of water wheels, or dynamos, would convert the water power into electrical power.

Although his plan did get as far as Albany, the state capital, Alonzo's dream did not materialize. But he did not give up, and in 1919 was pushing for what he called a "peace" bridge—one that would symbolically link two peaceful neighbours. In 1927, the 1700-metre, five-span Peace Bridge opened for traffic and soon became the busiest border crossing between the two countries. In 1992, a plan to build a new structure that would have increased traffic flow by 33 percent, fell victim to court challenges, with motorists continuing to face numbing line-ups to cross.

To honour the man whose vision of the peaceful link between neighbours finally found form in the Peace Bridge, in 1939 the Niagara Parks Commission constructed a triple-arch stone monument in Fort Erie near the western entrance to the Peace Bridge. Dedicated in 1940, the monument is surrounded by a garden within view of Mather's bridge. Mather died in California in 1941. He was 97.

99

A memorial arch in Fort Erie dedicated to Alonzo Mather
frames the Peace Bridge, which he had promoted.

THE *KEEWATIN* IS HOME

100

Port McNicoll

AFTER NEARLY FOUR decades in American waters, the CPR steamship the SS *Keewatin* is back home in Port McNicoll.

Built in Scotland in 1907, the *Keewatin* went into service the next year. Along with four other ships, the *Keewatin* linked the ports of southern Georgian Bay with the lakehead at Port Arthur for sixty years.

Operating originally from Owen Sound, where the CPR's Georgian Bay terminus lay, the ship relocated to Port McNicoll in 1912, once the CPR had completed its Sudbury main line.

More than 120 metres long, the mighty *Titanic*-like vessel could accommodate 280 passengers and carried a crew of 86. From Port McNicoll, the cruise took two and a half days and often stopped in various north Georgian Bay ports to off-load freight as well as local residents.

But times and regulations were changing. Following the tragic *Noronic* fire of 1949, where nearly 140 sleeping passengers burned to death or drowned while jumping to safety as the ship lay berthed in Toronto harbour, the government began to tighten regulations. In 1965, the *Keewatin* sailed its last cruise.

After fire consumed its sister ship the *Assiboine* in 1968, the *Keewatin* became the last Edwardian ship afloat on the Great Lakes and it, too, appeared destined for the scrapyard. But in 1967, a Great Lakes historian, R. J. Patterson of Douglas, Michigan, rescued the historic ship, towing it to the Kalamazoo River on Lake Michigan. There he converted it to a floating museum.

Then, in 2012, a Port McNicoll group, the Friends of the *Keewatin*, purchased the ship and began preparations for its return to Port McNicoll. Later that year, the ship opened for tours.

Comparisons to the *Titanic* were not out of place. Elaborate staircases with railings of carved wood lead from the main deck to the flower pot lounge at stateroom level.

All features are now displayed on the volunteer-led tour. Those tours include all portions of the mighty ship. Everything remains original to its later years, including staterooms, crew quarters, the wheelhouse and even the grain holds and the mighty boilers. Be sure to stand on the bow and gaze out toward the endless waters of Georgian Bay, much as the passengers might have done in the ship's bustling heyday.

Launched in 1907, the majestic *Keewatin* is now home in Port McNicoll. It displayed luxurious trappings (inset) similar to those of the ill-fated Titanic.

THE HOOKERS OF PORT CREDIT

101

(Stone-Hookers, That Is)

UNLIKE THAT OTHER profession, the stone-hooking trade in Ontario is now all but forgotten. After the middle of the nineteenth century, demand for construction material skyrocketed. Cities and towns, especially those around the growing city of Toronto, were expanding along with demand for more roads and rail lines. The most readily available materials for construction were the many rocks and boulders, particularly well rounded and often flat shale, that lined the shore of Lake Ontario.

Beginning in the 1840s, stone-hooker boats would depart the many ports along Lake Ontario from Whitby to Port Credit. These would usually be manned by four men with grappling hooks to lift the stones onto the barge. The stone loads, known as toises, were then transferred onto to schooners for the trip to the wharfs in Toronto, where they would be sorted by size according to use. Smaller stones would be used for road ballast, flat stones for pavement, while large round rocks would end up in building foundations.

By the 1850s, more than thirty stone boats were wrenching the rocks from the waters. With their shallow drafts, the boats could manoeuvre close to the shore — too close, it seems. Farmers began to complain that the operations were causing their farmland to erode and, in 1857, new laws required that operations take place no closer than 30 metres from shore.

But concrete soon replaced the stones in construction and, by the outbreak of the First World War, fewer than a half-dozen stone boats remained in use.

Nearly all vestiges of the trade have vanished. One exception is a small stone building at 49 Bronte Road in the old village of Bronte, formerly a popular restaurant known as Stoneboats and constructed from these stones by a one-time stone boat captain. Other buildings in the vicinity, such as the historic Glendella House, display those lake stone foundations.

Stones grappled from the waters of Lake Ontario have been used in local buildings in the Bronte area.

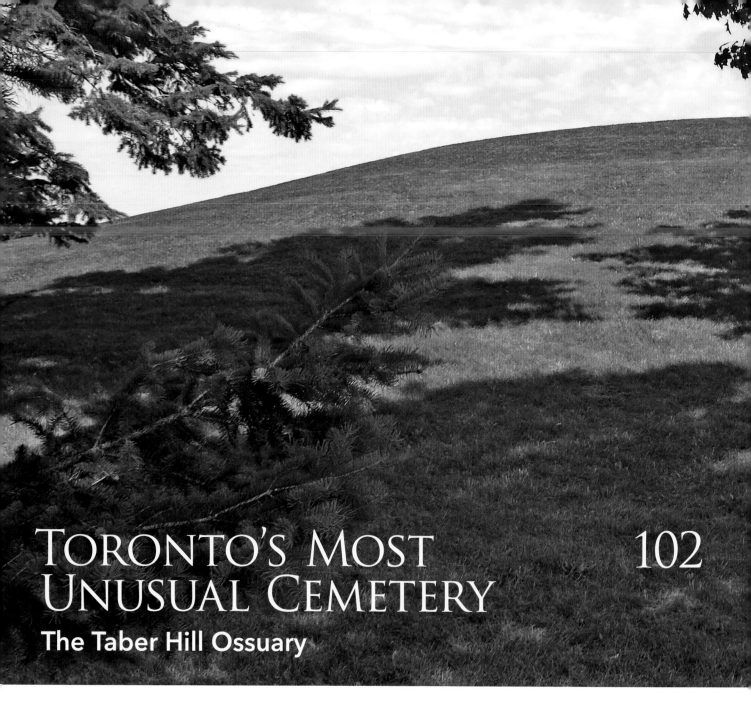

TORONTO'S MOST UNUSUAL CEMETERY
The Taber Hill Ossuary

102

I N THE HEART of suburban Scarborough, surrounded by curving streets and '60s-era back-splits, there rises Taber Hill, an unusual smooth mound, with a large granite boulder resting on top. It is not a natural feature. Rather, the mound contains the remains of nearly 500 Iroquois bodies buried sometime during the fourteenth century, well before the first Europeans had landed on mainland Canada.

Fast forward six centuries, and the farm fields of the rural township of Scarborough were in the throes of a suburban boom.

Corn fields were being bulldozed for new homes, and Highway 401 was making its way around the then northern limits of Toronto. While digging up earth in 1956 for a 401 overpass and to make way for new housing, a steam shovel operator looked in surprise to see parts of human skeletons on his shovel.

Province of Ontario archaeologists quickly made their way to the scene and recommended the province acquire the site and declare it a cemetery. Although Iroquois left their dead in trees, they would

218

TABER HILL
SITE OF AN ANCIENT INDIAN OSSUARY
OF THE IROQUOIS NATION
BURIALS WERE MADE ABOUT 1250 AND THIS
OSSUARY WAS UNCOVERED WHEN FARM
LANDS WERE DEVELOPED INTO
RESIDENTIAL PROPERTIES IN 1956
THIS COMMON GRAVE CONTAINS THE
REMAINS OF
APPROXIMATELY 472 PERSONS.

DEDICATED AS A HISTORICAL SITE BY
THE TOWNSHIP OF SCARBOROUGH
OCTOBER 21, 1961

later collect the bodies for a mass burial. Another documented ossuary lies north of Barrie, Ontario, while the remains of an Iroquois village were unearthed close by the Taber Hill site.

In 1961, local dignitaries and First Nations representatives participated in a Feast of the Dead ceremony. Today, a large granite boulder with an historical plaque on one side and an Iroquois prayer dominates the hilltop. The ossuary is prominently situated on Bellamy Road, between Eglinton Avenue and Lawrence Avenue.

An unusual mound in the heart of suburban Scarborough is in fact an ancient Aboriginal ossuary or burial mound.

Inset: A plaque atop the Taber Hill ossuary displays a First Nations poem.

219

COTTAGE COUNTRY
& NORTHERN ONTARIO

COTTAGE COUNTRY
& NORTHERN ONTARIO

James Bay

N

Moosonee **109**

ONR

Kenora

17

Hearst **113** Kapuskasing **11** Cochrane

105

ACR

Larder Lake **123**

106 White River

112 **11**

Rainy River

Thunder Bay **124**

111 **103**

125

107 Chapleau

Lake Superior

116 VIA Rail

17

Sault Ste Marie

17 **115** Sudbury

122 **108**

Manitoulin Island

Algonquin Park

11

New Liskeard

Temagami **119**

North Bay

17

114

Parry Sound

120

104

121 Huntsville

118

117

400

110 **11**

Map not to scale

NICHOLSON

A Ghost Town Worth Visiting

103

THE PROVINCE OF Quebec can boast about its ghost-town park of Val Jalbert, while the state of Michigan can claim Fayette. But Ontario, with its many ghost towns, can make no such claim. Although it once came close.

Nicholson came from the vision of two determined entrepreneurs. Northerners James Austin and George Nicholson from Chapleau, a railway centre and the site of a sawmill, recognized the growing demand for timber for railway ties. On the shore of Windermere Lake, about 19 kilometres west of Chapleau, they built a mill to manufacture such ties. The bustling town, with two churches, a hotel, a store, a

school and a boarding house, was for three decades home to 250 residents. When the mill burned in 1933, the town was largely abandoned.

Forty years later, a team of Ontario government historians visited the site. They parted the bushes and stared at the abandoned main street and overgrown cabins of the once-thriving town. The sight so impressed them that they recommended that Nicholson be preserved as a ghost-town park.

That might have happened except for two critical factors. First, the government department to which the historians reported was the Ontario Ministry of

The ghost town of Nicholson almost became a ghost-town park.

Natural Resources. Regarding the project as beyond its scope, the ministry ignored the recommendation. Then, shortly after the report was relegated to the shelves, a careless hunter accidentally set one of the flimsy structures ablaze. The ensuing inferno consumed most of what had been the main street, and with it, Ontario's hopes of having a ghost-town park.

Despite the destruction, the site remains one of the province's most striking ghost towns. Several of the old cabins can still be found, in use now as cottages. Others lie long abandoned, collapsing in

the advancing forest. Visible, too, are the two-storey school and the former Catholic church, although both are now in a collapsed state.

Although it is possible to reach the site by VIA Rail's Sudbury-to-White River rail-liner, schedules no longer permit a same-day return. The simpler route to the site is by boat from Shoals Provincial Park, located on the south side of the lake.

If provincial decision-makers had acted years ago, Ontario, like Quebec and Michigan, could claim its own ghost-town park. Today, it's too late.

DYER'S DEDICATION 104
Muskoka's Wilderness Memorial

CALLING MUSKOKA A "wilderness" anymore may be a stretch. With lakeside condos and country homes, it is now more a form of low-density sprawl enhanced by lakes and woodlands. But as you negotiate your car along the narrow road that leads to the Dyer Memorial, north of Huntsville, and the trees on either side close in, you might be forgiven for thinking that you are indeed in the wilds.

That's what it was when Clifton G. Dyer and his wife, Betsy, began visiting the area. They spent their honeymoon canoeing in Algonquin Park in 1916 and fell in love with the land. In 1940 they built a cottage on the Big East River, near Huntsville, returning every year to that wilderness retreat until 1956, when Betsy died.

Dyer was devoted to his wife, and in the year after her death he built a moving tribute to her. On the highest point on his property, overlooking their beloved river, he erected a 12-metre stone cairn. He surrounded it with a 390-square-metre flagstone terrace, and around that created a 4-hectare botanical garden. On the top of the cairn, in a copper urn, he placed his wife's ashes to rest. Following his own death, in 1959, his ashes were placed next to hers.

Although the public enjoys free access, Dyer's Memorial is on private property. The Dyer estate, which still maintains the cairn and garden, welcomes visitors, who in the summer may number two hundred a day. The memorial is located near the hamlet of Williamsport, about 10 kilometres northeast of Huntsville. Small arrows point the way.

Although Clifton Dyer's cottage was sold long ago, the wilderness memorial to his wife will survive with his dedication to her: "An affectionate, loyal and understanding wife is life's greatest gift."

Dyer's wilderness memorial.

105

The log White Otter Castle was built by one man alone in the bush.

THE LOG CASTLE ON WHITE OTTER LAKE

THOSE THINGS THAT are the hardest to reach often offer the richest rewards. So is the case with the strange log castle on White Otter Lake, some 64 kilometres north of Atikokan, in northwestern Ontario. Accessible only by boat, float plane or four-wheel drive, this three-storey mansion was constructed entirely of red pine logs by a wiry little man only 5 foot 7 inches, with no help and no machinery.

In 1887, James McQuat arrived from Scotland to carve out a farm in the wilderness of northwestern Ontario. A decade of inconsistent crops followed. Then came the cry "gold!" The northwestern Ontario gold rush was on, and McQuat joined the stampede into the bush. But he fared no better at prospecting than he had at farming. Determined to show his worth to society and, it is said, to attract the love of a lady, McQuat decided to build a castle. He chose a sand beach on the northwest arm of White Otter Lake. Here, facing west, he could enjoy his favourite image, the spectacular northwestern sunset.

He carefully chose the finest logs, hand winched them through the bush, squared them on three sides, and carefully dovetailed the ends to make an airtight fit. By using skids, holes and pegs, McQuat patiently and painstakingly inched the logs up the walls, until finally his tower stood four storeys high and measured more than 3 metres square at the base. The main house was three storeys high and 7 metres square, while a further two-storey addition at the back served as his living quarters.

Contrary to later legend, McQuat was neither a hermit nor an eccentric. Rather, he enjoyed company and travelled frequently to the busy railway town of Ignace, the nearest supply point, and often showed off photographs of his home.

The irony was that his castle was never his own, for he had squatted on Crown land. For three years he carried on a futile effort to acquire the title, but the Department of Lands and Forests repeatedly denied his requests. His dispute abruptly ended when on October 8, 1920, he become entangled in his fishing nets only metres away from his castle and drowned. He was fifty-eight years old.

For seven decades his castle has stood empty, damaged by water but generally free from vandals. In 1955 the department added concrete foundations, new roofing and better bracing. It was later more fully restored by the Friends of White Otter.

You can reach White Otter Castle from a number of fishing camps on the lake, or by boat from Clearwater Lake on Highway 622. And as you watch the sun set over the quiet, northern lake, you will understand why Jimmy McQuat called it home.

GRAND CANYON NORTH

106

Ouimet Canyon

I't's little wonder that Group of Seven painters A. Y. Jackson, Franklin Carmichael and Lawren Harris fell in love with Superior country. Nearly every bend in its rivers and nearly every bay in its lakes displays a panorama of mountain scenery that is as unexpected as it is awesome. And when, at the end of a trail through a pine forest near Nipigon, Ontario, the land drops away, unannounced, at your feet, to reveal a sudden and magnificent canyon, you understand how scenery can be called "unexpected."

As a tourist attraction, Ouimet Canyon Provincial Park is relatively unknown. No motels have sprung up to accommodate the hoards, no gift shops line the roads. Most Trans-Canada Highway travellers simply ignore the simple brown sign that points the way. But as a visual spectacle, Ouimet Canyon is breathtaking and unique.

The craggy crevice, 150 metres wide and 100 deep, twists several kilometres north from the lip of the grand plateau into which it has been cut. So little sunshine penetrates the deep gully that winter ice can linger into summer, and only hardy Arctic species of mosses, lichens and liverworts can survive.

The canyon traces its origins back to the last great ice age, when glaciers 2 kilometres thick crept southward, scouring and gouging everything in their path. Here at Ouimet Canyon, a tongue of ice crept down what was an eroded diabase sill. That diabase was formed a billion years ago when magma rose to the surface, creating the pillar-like formations that line the valley walls. Some of those pillars, owing to erosion, are free-standing.

The road to Ouimet Canyon from the Trans-Canada Highway (about 55 kilometres east of Thunder Bay) passes some surprisingly lush farmland before twisting its way up the face of the rocky plateau. From the parking lot in the provincial park an easy trail winds through the forest for about a kilometre up to the rim of the canyon.

From the viewing areas, the panorama encompasses not only the defile itself but also its rugged gates at the rim of the plateau, the forested lands beyond, and along the far horizon the grey waters of Lake Superior.

As you gaze at the results of nature's remarkable strength, as the northern stillness rings in your ears, and as the sharp, pine-scented air stings your nostrils, you will understand why the Group of Seven kept coming back.

Ontario's miniature version of the Grand Canyon, Ouimet Canyon, is so deep and narrow that plants otherwise native to the Arctic thrive in its dark recesses.

THE ALGOMA CENTRAL
A Train Ride from the Past

AS THE FIRST rays of sunrise brighten the streets of Hearst, bleary-eyed tourists begin to wander to the platform of the Algoma Central Railway (ACR) station. Awaiting them on the tracks are the two passenger cars of ACR's Train 632, also known as the "Milk Run." They are about to embark on one of the last of the old-style train rides in Canada.

Not a museum train, 632 is all utilitarian. The 476-kilometre line between the sleepy sawmill town of Hearst and the bustling industrial city of Sault Ste. Marie is populated by prospectors, loggers, trappers, cottagers and campers, all dependent upon this train to link them with the "outside."

Throughout the ride, the train often stops on demand. At Wabatong, a wooden "umbrella" station beside Wabatong Lake, cottagers and fishermen climb on board. At Oba, a community of one hundred still entirely dependent on rail access, parcels and freight are hand loaded on or off the mail car. Further down the line, another rail-dependent village, Franz, now nearly a ghost town, is the ACR's junction with the CPR.

The morning hours of the southbound are spent hurtling through a low spruce forest that is flat and dreary, but includes the "floating" bridges of Oba Lake, built on pilings driven into the seemingly bottomless muskeg. Later, during the afternoon, spectacular cliffs loom above a foaming stream as the train enters the Agawa Canyon. This ancient and spectacular defile is the destination of the internationally popular tourist trains, the longest in the world, that depart daily from Sault Ste. Marie. But unlike the tourist trains, the Milk Run does not stop to allow for an afternoon of picnicking and hiking.

Throughout the trip, which can last up to ten hours, an easy joviality permeates the train. Tourists gape at the passing landscape, while cottagers, campers and canoeists scramble on at the many flag stops, as acquaintances are renewed and familiar chatter fills the coaches. The busiest stop en route is the two-storey station at Hawk Junction. Travellers embarking in Sault Ste. Marie will need to purchase their tickets at the downtown station, although the train itself departs only from a featureless parking lot at the north end of the CN yards.

Visitors should check the Algoma Central website (www.agawacanyontourtrain.com) for the most recent schedule.

107

Passengers get ready to board the local train at Hawk Junction station.

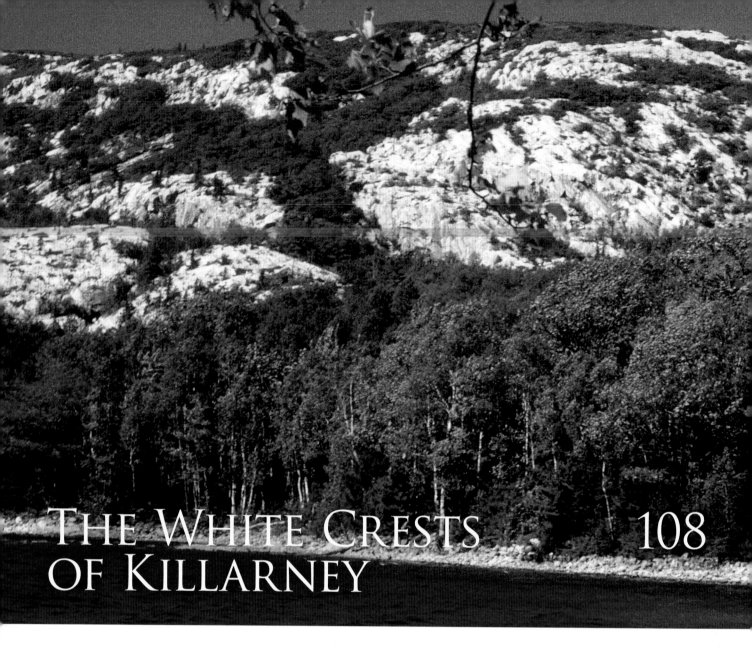

THE WHITE CRESTS OF KILLARNEY

108

DRIVING WEST ON Highway 637, just south of Sudbury, you soon see the domes of white, gleaming above the low, green forest. Your first thoughts are that freak weather has preserved a mountain of snow into the summer season. But as you drive closer you realize that these are the legendary La Cloche Mountains of Killarney, and the "snow" is quartzite rock of pure white.

About two billion years ago an ancient sea laid down a bed of sand that was unusually rich in silica. As the shifting bedrock hurled the seabed into a giant mountain range, the layers of silica were compressed into masses of white quartzite, forming a mountain range loftier than today's Rockies. Eons of rain, wind and grinding glaciers eroded the peaks into the round, white knobs that today provide the spectacular backdrop for the northern shores of Georgian Bay and Lake Huron. The white wall of mountains stretches in a thin line for about 60 kilometres and soars in places to heights of 500 metres.

The early French explorers gave the mountains their word for "bell," because they reported that certain rocks, when struck, echoed like a bell.

The area's early history has little to do with the scenery. Following the days when Killarney was a stopover for Native

The pure white quartzite rocks of the Killarney mountains resemble a hillside of snow.

and French-Canadian fur traders, logging companies began to strip the pine from the mountainsides. The village of Killarney, now dependent upon tourism for its survival, originated as a fur-trading post and fishing village.

But it was the scenery that attracted the area's earliest tourists. Among them were a pair of young painters named Franklin Carmichael and A. Y. Jackson, whose works *Summer Storm*, *Bay of Islands* and *Nellie Lake* are among the most prized Group of Seven works. Their works in part inspired the Ontario government to create

the much-visited Killarney Provincial Park, with its campsites, canoe routes and hiking trails, one of which is 100 kilometres long.

The park is 70 kilometres west of Highway 69 along Highway 637.

You can also travel by boat to Killarney and explore the mountain-lined fjords. Or you can approach the mountains on Highway 6 south of Espanola to a soaring pass over the Tower Mountain summit near Willisville. But regardless of how you get there, the La Cloche Mountains of Killarney remain one of the most unusual alpine destinations east of the Rockies.

MOOSE FACTORY'S FLOATING CHURCH

109

LOCATED ON A desolate island in the Moose River, close to its mouth on James Bay, Moose Factory is claimed to be Ontario's oldest permanent settlement. The Company of Gentlemen Adventurers Trading into Hudson's Bay opened several posts across northern Canada. In 1673, they established Moose Fort, as the settlement was then called.

With the major European powers fighting for control of North America, ownership of Moose Factory alternated between the French and the English. By the time the Hudson's Bay Company and its rival, the North West Company, merged in 1821, the fighting had ended and Moose Fort became Moose Factory.

Between this time and the arrival in 1930 of the Temiskaming and Northern Ontario Railway at Moosonee on the mainland, the company added a number of new buildings to the trading post. The officers' dwelling was constructed in 1847; a building erected to house the fur trader's interpreter, a Cree of mixed ancestry named Joseph Turner, appeared in 1864; and the home belonging to the company carpenter, William McLeod, was added in 1889. One of the oldest buildings still standing is the company blacksmith shop, built around 1850. The shop operated until 1934.

And then there was St. Thomas Anglican Church, fondly known as the "floating church." While it does not literally "float," the building was so prone to inundations from the river that special plugs were incorporated into the floorboards that could be removed in order to let the water come in. Otherwise the surging flood waters could seriously damage the church's foundations, or even lift it up and float it away.

Its first pastor, the Reverend John Horden, was the first to translate hymns, prayers and many passages from the Bible into the Cree syllables previously devised by John Evans.

The white frame church, with its slender spire, also contains a collection of attractive stained-glass windows. The nearby graveyard holds markers that date back to 1802.

While the Hudson's Bay Company moved away in 1989, the Ontario Heritage Foundation and the Moose Cree First Nation have worked to save many of the island's historic fur-trading buildings. The island is accessible by Cree freighter canoe or through Kway Journey Tours from Moosonee, the Ontario Northland Railway's terminus for the popular Polar Bear Express tourist train.

Moose Factory's Anglican church was built with holes in the floor to prevent the frequent floodwaters from floating it away.

BOATS ON RAILS
The Big Chute Marine Railway

THE GROANING LIFT locks at Peterborough and Kirkfield are not the only unusual structures on the Trent-Severn Waterway. About 40 kilometres north of Barrie, County Road 24 leaves the village of Coldwater and takes you 20 kilometres along a winding road, past farms and through forests to the Big Chute Marine Railway.

By the turn of the century, urbanites, fed up with the noise and fumes of the industrial cities, were finding a tranquil escape at places like the mouth of the Severn River. By 1906 there was increasing pressure to open up still more of the Severn, and the federal government gave approval to a marine railway that would guide the boats over the steep falls known as the Big Chute (a temporary railway already existed for workers then constructing a hydro generator station at the same location).

In 1920 the marine railway was finished, but by 1922 it needed enlarging. The new car was 4 metres wide by 11 metres long. It operated by being lowered into the water at one end, where the boats could be floated over the carriage and secured. The carriage was then winched out of the water and pulled along rails to the height of land where the cables were manually switched for the descent into the water at the other end.

Following the Second World War, recreational boating experienced an unprecedented boom. By the 1970s the outdated marine railway had become such a bottleneck that considerable enlargement was necessary. In 1977 a new carriage, 13 metres wide and 36 metres long, began to rumble up and down the granite cliff. Unlike the old car, the new carriage uses a modern system of four winches operated by digital control and automatic cable transfer. The older historic car is still used to handle overflow.

Viewing is easy. Parks Canada has created an attractive park with hiking and picnicking facilities. Amid the benches you may see concrete steps. These once led to the large houses that were home to the original workers in the hydroelectric plant. But it's the sight of a luxury yacht creaking up a cliff on a railway car that you won't easily forget.

The site can now also be reached by following Muskoka Road 34 east from Highway 400.at Exit 156, just north of Port Severn.

A more modern carriage now carries boats up the steep
incline at the Big Chute on the Trent-Severn Canal.

These unexplained excavations are found throughout Ontario.

THOSE PERPLEXING PUKASKWA PITS

SOME OF ONTARIO's most unusual places predate recorded history. Early inhabitants left behind mounds, pits and paintings, features that filled crucial roles in their lives, but left question marks for a modern generation. While today's archaeologists may understand the paintings and the petroglyphs, no one has yet unravelled the mystery of the pukaskwa pits.

Found primarily around the shores of Lake Superior, pukaskwa pits (pronounced puk-a-saw) are manmade excavations dug into boulder beaches, which formed when the lake waters were about 30 metres higher than they are today. The conical pits are 2 or 3 metres across, with excavated stones piled protectively around the rim. Although clearly manmade, the lack of other evidence of human occupation, such as burial mounds, dumps or habitation areas, heightens their mystery. Archaeologists have found only bits of pottery, flints and caribou bones, suggesting that the use of the pits was likely short-lived.

One theory suggests that they were vision pits. Young men of each tribe isolated themselves until the spirit of the animal that guided their lives visited them. Others speculate that the pits were shelters from the storm-tossed waters of the lake during the peak of the fur trade. Their location,

close to the water but away from the waves, makes them excellent shelters for canoeists. Huddled inside, one is protected from the cold winds, while soaking up the sun. Some of the larger pits appear to have had hearths and possibly protective coverings.

The greatest concentration of pukaskwa pits is found along the northeastern shore of Lake Superior, where more than 250 are protected in Pukaskwa National Park. Because they can be easily altered, or even destroyed by accident or carelessness, their exact locations are not published. Pukaskwa Park epitomizes Northern Ontario. Mountain peaks soar 640 metres high, wild rivers plunge through steep canyons, dense forests cloak the steep hillsides, and waves thunder against a rocky shore where cliffs loom high above the grey waters.

The park is accessed from Highway 17 by following Highway 627 through Heron Bay. Here you find the Friends of Pukaskwa store. From the campground and visitor centre, a 60-kilometre hiking trail leads along the coast to its end at Hattie Bay. A well-travelled canoe route follows the shore, with campsites at several locations. And although the locations of the mystery pits are not given, those who hike or canoe the shoreline of the park will quickly find a few of these mysterious holes and ponder their origin.

Emo's Unusual Norlund Chapel

MANY CHURCHES HAVE lost their steeples, sometimes to fire, sometimes to old age. But the Norlund Chapel in Emo, Ontario, is a steeple that has lost its church.

Emo is located in the far northwestern reaches of Ontario. Here, the surprising land is flat and the soil is black and almost treeless. Geologically, this part of Ontario is an extension of the prairie landscape. To reach this rich land, the first settlers travelled along the wide Rainy River by steamer. Along the way villages grew up around the many little steamer landings. In 1904, the railway arrived, eliminating the role of many of the steamer villages.

Midway between the railway towns of Fort Frances and Rainy River, Emo got a station and became a busy town. But its origins as a steamer stop remain visible, with a main street that developed along the riverfront. As it grew, Emo attracted businesses, schools and churches. In 1935, St. Patrick's Roman Catholic Church was built on the outskirts of the village. Its 12-metre-high wooden steeple was topped with a 2-metre-high wrought-iron cross fashioned by a local blacksmith.

In 1971, lightning struck and destroyed the church. Incredibly, the steeple survived, nearly unscathed. To celebrate the miracle, Elmer Norlund and Ed Sletmoen designed a chapel around the steeple. Its diminutive size, just 2 metres by 3, is barely enough to allow eight people to fill the building. Now nondenominational, it is open to worshippers of all faiths. The Norlund Chapel with its Emo steeple is one of the world's smallest churches, and can be found on the north side of Highway 11/71 at the village limits.

Norlund Church in Emo – a steeple without a church.

112

This Northern Ontario monument recalls a tragic labour dispute.

Monument to Murder
Massacre at Reesor Siding

Unlike the more popular Trans-Canada Highway, which follows the spectacular shore of Lake Superior, there is another "trans-Canada highway." Numbered as Highway 11, it passes through northeastern Ontario, offering landscapes that are much less dramatic. Much of it traverses the northern Clay Belt, where sleepy railway towns appear at regular intervals throughout the flat farmlands. It comes as a surprise then to see above an overgrown field a monument to a murder.

In January of 1963, more than one thousand members of the Lumber and Sawmill Workers Union working in eight bush camps staged a wildcat strike to protest the slow progress of contract talks with the Spruce Falls pulp mill in Kapuskasing. But they weren't the only suppliers of logs. Local farmers also hauled logs from their own lots as independent contractors, and they had no affiliation with the union. Suspicious of unions, they refused to support the strike and continued to pile their logs at nearby Reesor Siding for shipment to the mill.

Tensions ran high. The company refused to negotiate until the workers returned to the camps. The workers refused to return until the company began to negotiate. Calls for the provincial government to appoint a conciliator went unheeded. The government then made the situation worse by granting permits to the independent farmers to continue to supply logs. Frustrated by the lack of progress, and angered by the farmers' antipathy, the strikers began to vandalize the log piles at the siding

On the night of February 11, four hundred strikers marched on the siding to once again unpile the logs. Alerted by the police, the farmers, now armed, huddled in a cabin waiting for them. Shots rang out in the cold night air and three strikers fell dead. Another eight lay wounded.

Twenty of the farmers were brought to trial, charged with "non-capital" murder. Without proof of who fired the guns, they were acquitted. Meanwhile, more than two hundred strikers were convicted of participating in a riot and fined. To commemorate the tragic deaths of the union strikers, the United Brotherhood of Carpenters and Joiners has erected a large monument, which rises incongruously above the flat landscape of the deserted siding and speaks for itself. In a fitting act of irony, the workers now own the mill.

The monument looms above a field on Highway 11, 50 kilometres west of Kapuskasing.

ALGONQUIN PARK'S INCREDIBLE BARRON CANYON

114

AT FIRST GLANCE it is hard to believe that Ontario has a canyon so deep and so precipitous. While the magnificent Ouimet Canyon in Northern Ontario is longer and wider and displays a collection of rare Arctic plants, the canyon on the Barron River in northeastern Algonquin Park is both narrower and considerably deeper.

Its origins are as unique as the canyon itself. After the rocks of the Canadian Shield were formed billions of years ago, they lay buried beneath the deposits of an ancient sea. Under the waters of that sea, the sandy deposits gradually hardened into limestone. When the entire area heaved upward, the limestone cap fragmented into fault lines that ran in a northwest to southeast direction.

Millions of centuries later, as the great ice sheets that covered Ontario retreated northward, the meltwaters drained along the fault lines. One channel became the outlet for an enormous post-glacial lake named Lake Algonquin. Some geologists estimate that the torrent equalled a thousand Niagaras, one of which gradually carved out the Barron Canyon. As the ice sheet continued its northerly retreat, the meltwaters found a lower outlet that became the Mattawa and Ottawa rivers.

Since then, erosion has continued its sculpting magic on the canyon. The harsh freeze-and-thaw action of the frigid Algonquin winters causes chunks of rock to fragment and cascade into the valley far below.

For a few decades the Barron River echoed to the shouts of loggers pushing their logs downstream to mills at Petawawa and Pembroke. After the last drive ended in 1936, the cleft became an awe-inspiring destination for canoeists and hikers. Bird-watchers observed such unlikely species as the swamp-loving yellow-bellied flycatcher and the common yellowthroat along the cliffs, as well as rare bald eagles.

Thanks to Algonquin's park planners, the canyon is easy to visit and photograph. From the parking area 11 kilometres west of the Sand Lake gate, a 1.5-kilometre loop trail leads to the lip of the precipice, a dizzying 100 metres above the river below. The trail is occasionally steep and the edge unfenced. From the top, breathtaking views extend far downstream to the east. Canoes can launch at a number of landings.

The portion of the river between the soaring walls is relatively placid, with only a few portages, and makes for a pleasant afternoon to view one of Ontario's more unusual and spectacular geological wonders.

The dizzying Barron River canyon is the most spectacular chasm in Ontario.

A Green Sudbury

COULD THE BARREN moonscape once described as one of the world's worst environmental disasters ever be green again? So barren was the soil of Sudbury that American astronauts practised their moonwalks on the tormented terrain.

A century ago Sudbury was green. Pine forest covered the granite rocks. In 1883, the Canadian Pacific Railway blasted these rocks to make way for the national dream of a rail line to the Pacific, and the discovery of the world's largest deposit of copper and nickel in those rock cuts turned the little railway junction into a major mining town. But nickel refining is also one of the most polluting industries.

An obsolete process called "roasting" caused the damage. Crushed ore was laid on vast beds of burning cordwood. The roasting beds burned for months, sending billowing clouds of sulphur-laden smoke across the landscape. The smoke killed everything it touched. The refinery stacks were even worse, spewing tiny particles of nickel and copper oxide, which seeped into and poisoned the ground.

Trees were killed in all directions. The ground was barren. Nothing grew in the poisoned terrain.

Then, in 1969, when Inco constructed a superstack to spread the fumes further afield, local residents decided to make Sudbury green again. Although the first efforts at reforestation on the infertile ground were dismal failures, a few years later a Laurentian University biology professor began to experiment with lime. By laying down a layer of lime first, the poisons were neutralized. A variety of grasses were then planted. Once the grass took hold, the trees followed.

Schoolchildren, youth and miners all clambered over the hillsides and tailings, planting trees by the thousands. The efforts have won several national and international awards, including the Lieutenant Governor's Conservation Award, the United States Chevron Conservation Award, and the United Nations Local Government Honours Award, presented at the Earth Summit in Rio de Janeiro.

In 1997, the regional municipality unveiled a plaque beside its premier landmark, the Big Nickel, announcing the planting of the three millionth tree. Since that date, a further six million trees have been planted. Ironically, looming on the hill next to the plaque are the now-cleaned-up Inco stacks, and in between, a young forest of saplings that could only have been imagined a few years earlier.

115

Nine million trees have been replanted on what was
once a barren, polluted moonscape.

116

The main street of Missanabie is almost a ghost main street, yet a handful of residents still live here and travel by rail.

Top: The *Superior*, VIA Rail's "ghost-town train," passes the vanished mill town of Sheahan.

ONTARIO'S GHOST-TOWN TRAIN

THE FIRST LINE through Ontario's North Country was the Canadian Pacific. By the 1880s, its rails led through North Bay and Sudbury, steaming through the great pine forests. Along its route countless sawmills and villages for the workers grew up at trackside. By the 1930s, most of the timber supply was depleted, and the mills closed or burned. Those communities fortunate enough to attract other industries managed to struggle on. Most, however, simply died.

VIA's transcontinental trains were shifted from the CP line to the tracks of the Canadian National in 1990, but there remains a VIA service from Sudbury to White River and, along the route, the vestiges of several ghosted mill towns can be seen.

After departing Sudbury, the self-propelled chrome coaches rumble through the sprawling suburbs of mining towns with names like Levack, Onaping and Cartier. The first of the ghost towns comes up quickly—the half-dozen weathered trackside cabins of a former pulp-siding and mill town named Benny.

While it will not stop here or at the ghost town of Sheahan, where the mills of W. B. Plaunt's lumber company operated between 1929 and 1940, the train may halt at the ghost town of Metagama, where a few weathered section cabins still stand.

Perhaps the most prominent ghost town on the route is Biscotasing. Once a bustling sawmill town and home to the legendary "invented" Indian, Grey Owl, Biscotasing still boasts many of its original homes on the winding dirt streets. Looming high above the station shelter is the weathered ruin of the Roman Catholic church.

Next up is a vast meadow that, until the late 1970s, was the site of the Korpela and Maki mills that gave the place its name—Kormak. The mill and the town were removed in the 1970s.

After stopping for a break in the divisional town of Chapleau, the train once more enters the woods, where it quickly comes to the ghost town of Nicholson. Nicholson's railway tie mill burned in the 1930s, but much of the town remained intact until a fire in the mid-1970s destroyed a large part of the main street. Today the ruins can still be seen in the woods.

The train then rushes past cabins and a church—the remains of the mill town of Dalton Station. After stopping at the nearby town of Missinabie, it continues on to the one-time gold-mining town of Lochalsh. The remains of the town lie out of sight from the train, in the woods above the rail line.

The train ride ends at White River, another divisional town, returning to Sudbury the following day.

117

Woodchester Villa, Bracebridge

EIGHT SIDES TO A HOUSE
Woodchester Villa

DURING THE FIRST two generations of Ontario's European settlement, house styles were fairly uniform; from log cabins to Georgian mansions, the pattern was consistently boxy. But with affluence and stability, and with the increasing artistic curiosity of the Victorian age, there came more architectural experimentation. This brought one of the more unusual house styles ever seen in Ontario, and indeed in northeastern North America: the eight-sided house.

The origin of the design is credited to an amateur architect, American Orson Fowler, who featured it in his 1848 book, *A Home for All*. Its advantages, he argued, were that a greater floor-space-to-wall-space ratio made it cheaper to build. And with more external wall space for windows, it was brighter and therefore healthier.

Henry Bird apparently agreed. In 1882, he built one of Ontario's first octagonal houses, in what was then a raw frontier town named Bracebridge. The owner of a large woollen mill, Bird built his home near the pioneer Muskoka Road, on a hill overlooking the town. The eight walls alternated between 5 metres and 4.5 metres wide, and were nearly a half metre thick. The house remained in the Bird family for nearly a century, until it was sold to a local service club and shortly thereafter opened as a museum.

The style had many imitators, and by 1900 Ontario could boast more than one hundred octagonal houses. Today fewer than half remain, most in central or eastern Ontario, including in Lowville, Huttonville, Maple, Picton, Calabogie and Hawkesbury (which also claims an octagonal barn). Ontario's northernmost multi-sided building is a popular round barn near Sault Ste. Marie, on the Trans-Canada Highway.

Woodchester Villa is located on King Street, close to the historic alignment of the Muskoka Road, although the steepness of the hill here closed the through route.

In 2009, a winter storm damaged the aging building so severely that the Town of Bracebridge had no choice but to close it to the public. In 2013, the town council approved nearly $1 million to repair the tourist attraction.

A LEGACY IN LOG
The Madill Church

WHEN PIONEERS CLEARED the forests and broke the soil, their first buildings were hastily built of the closest material at hand—logs. Shanties had to make do until a larger, second home could be built, also of logs. Once the farmers became established they added their third house, now more substantial and built with stone, brick or planks.

Throughout most of Ontario, the log era has long passed. However, in the Ottawa Valley and the rugged uplands of Muskoka there remains a log legacy that includes barns, houses, churches, schools, general stores and hotels. Near Petawawa, west of Ottawa, stands a log hotel with its stables, all dating from the days of stage travel. Known as the Ferguson Stopping Place, it is now a bed and breakfast. On the grounds of the Waba Cottage Museum are a relocated log school and church.

A tour of almost any country road in the Ottawa Valley will reveal a form of barn known as the "string" barn. Where farmers could ill afford to replace their first log barns, they simply added to them, creating a string of barns that usually enclosed their animal pens.

The village of Burnstown, perched on a wall of the Madawaska River Canyon, boasts a log general store, while the village of Ashton can claim nearly half of its homes as log. Even Ottawa itself hides a pair of original log houses, both within a few paces of the popular downtown Byward Market.

Muskoka, too, celebrates its own log legacy with churches near Southwood, Bracebridge, Sand Lake and Rosseau; however, the best-known and most-visited is the Gothic log church founded by John Madill in 1873. It lies on the west side of the historic Muskoka Colonization Road at the Madill Church Road, a short distance west of Highway 11.

118

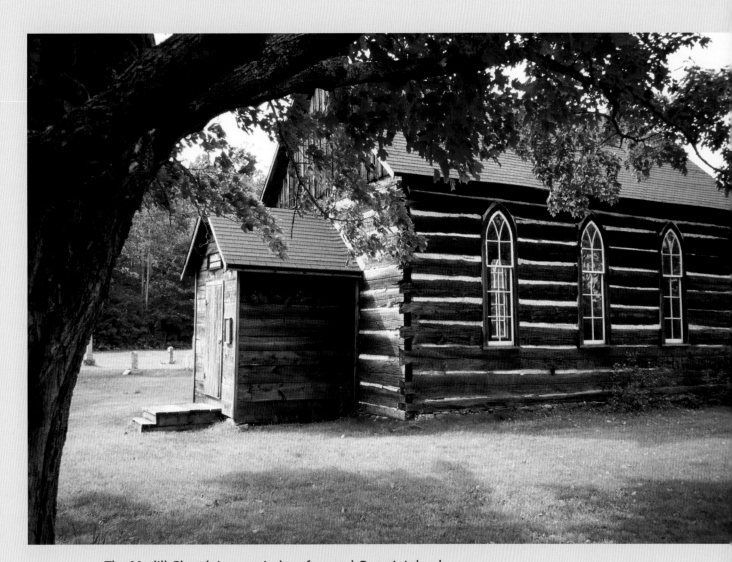

The Madill Church is a reminder of central Ontario's log legacy.

Temagami's Tall Pines

119

THE STATELY WHITE pine, Ontario's provincial tree, is threatened with extinction, thanks to the cutting plans devised by Ontario's Ministry of Natural Resources, along with the logging interests. The few remaining stands represent a mere 1 percent of the pine forest's original extent, and that makes them a rare heritage legacy. Many of those tall pines are to be found in the Temagami area of northeastern Ontario.

Situated about two hours' drive north of North Bay, the area contains a wilderness relic, with lakes and rivers surrounded by tall-pine forests. Of Temagami's tall-pine areas, the Lady Evelyn Smoothwater Park, accessible only by water, is perhaps the best known (although even it is now part of a ministry cutting plan).

A lesser-known tall-pine area, however, is easily accessible right within the limits of the village, and can be reached on foot. Known as the White Bear Forest, it takes its name from the last chief of a local tribe that used the area for hunting and trapping. In 1928, logging began on 500 square kilometres. But the company, run by the Gillies Brothers, decided to set aside the 800-hectare White Bear Forest as a reminder of what the ancient forests once looked like.

And it is here that the pines still loom large. The forest is the sixth largest old-growth white-pine forest still known, and, more remarkably, is the most accessible. Several kilometres of trail wind through the forest and can be accessed by car from the Caribou Mountain Ski Hill, or by boat from Northland Paradise Lodge on Snake Island Lake, which can also be reached by car. The trails range from one to two-and-a-half hours' hiking duration. While many ecological features dot the routes, from red-pine stands to beaver meadows, the highlight is the grove of soaring white pines on the north shore of Pleasant Lake (although they are found throughout the reserve). The forest also offers scenic lookouts and a preserved fire tower.

The village of Temagami, on Highway 11, contains a pair of small restaurants, a motel, access to several lodges, and a revitalized waterfront. The village's heritage centrepiece, however, is the historic Temiskaming & Northern Ontario (T&NO) railway station, restored by a local restoration trust. The Tudor-style stone station is one the most attractive in Northern Ontario. It continued to serve passengers travelling on the historic Northlander train until 2012, when the Ontario government cancelled the service.

The White Bear tall-pine forest at Temagami.

DEPOT HARBOUR
A Georgian Bay Ghost Port

120

DURING ITS HEYDAY, Depot Harbour was a busy railway terminus and Great Lakes port, and with sixteen hundred residents it threatened to eclipse places like Midland and Owen Sound. But today the wind blows across cracked sidewalks and overgrown foundations, as Georgian Bay's waves now lap against silent shores.

It all began in the 1890s, when lumber baron John Rudolphus Booth forged a rail link across the middle of Ontario. His Ottawa, Arnprior and Parry Sound Railway would not only access his rich pine forests, but would also give Canada's western grain growers their most direct route to the ice-free Atlantic Ocean ports.

A dispute over the location of the terminus on Georgian Bay led Booth to seek a site where he could build his own town. On Parry Island, beside the Great Lake's largest natural harbour, Booth built the town of Depot Harbour. The town contained three churches, a school, railway yards and a roundhouse, two large grain elevators and more than one hundred dwellings.

For three decades the place prospered. Then, in 1928, the Canadian National Railway, which had by then assembled a collection of bankrupt rail lines, amalgamated its facilities at a location south of Parry Sound. Five years later, an ice floe damaged a trestle in Algonquin Park and CN closed the route.

The lifeline of Depot Harbour was severed, a calamity from which it never recovered. In 1945, the port facilities, which were then storing the volatile cordite for a nearby munitions factory, erupted in a midnight fireball that lit up the streets of Parry Sound, 10 kilometres away. Depot Harbour's story was over. The houses were sold off for $25 each and moved away.

By the 1960s only the Catholic church, the shell of the roundhouse, and a single dwelling remained standing. Today, the roundhouse alone survives. Beyond it, hidden by a forest now a half century old, lie the foundations, the old sidewalks, the remains of the company vault, and the massive wharf, all now silent. Although the ruins become more and more obscured as the years pass, it remains Ontario's most extensive ghost town. In 1996, the townsite reverted to the ownership of the Wasauksing First Nation.

To reach Depot Harbour, follow the Rose Point Road from Parry Sound across the railway bridge to a T intersection. The ghost town is down a side trail, about 5 kilometres to the west.

The grey arches of a one-time railway roundhouse peer from the woods at the site of the once bustling port of Depot Harbour.

121

The historic *Portage Flyer* is ready to ride again.

THE RETURN OF MUSKOKA'S PORTAGE FLYER
The World's Shortest Railway

IT HAS COME back home. Following an absence of more than forty years, the famed *Portage Flyer* has returned to Muskoka. Once deemed the world's shortest commercial railway, the Huntsville and Lake of Bays Railway was a fixture on the landscape from 1904, when it began shuttling steamboat passengers between Peninsula Lake and Lake of Bays.

Although the Muskoka Lakes region had become a haven for tourists, roads and cars were many years in the future. Travellers would arrive by train and then transfer onto steamers for the trip to the many grand hotels that ringed the lakes. While vacationers could transfer easily from the Grand Trunk trains in Huntsville onto steamers bound for Fairy and Peninsula lakes, there remained a difficult height of land barring the route to the lovely Lake of Bays. A plan to connect Bracebridge to the lake by rail was scrapped when the steamboat company decided to link the lakes with a much shorter portage railway.

The narrow line had to climb more than 40 metres, doing so in just 3 kilometres. A pair of steam locomotives hauled two passenger coaches, which were converted from old Toronto streetcars. These were replaced in 1948 by newer engines. But the end of the era was in sight, and a decade later the Muskoka District had been infiltrated by new paved roads. Rather than taking steamers to lodges, city dwellers were packing their cars and driving to private cottages instead.

Steamers were floated into dry docks and scrapped; lodges were burned or demolished, and in 1959, the *Portage Flyer* made its last run. The equipment was sold and removed to Pinafore Park in St. Thomas, where it was a popular attraction. Finally, in 1984, the volunteer-run Huntsville and Lake of Bays Railway Society bought the old rolling stock and brought it back to Huntsville.

Finally, on June 1, 2000, the *Portage Flyer* once more puffed into service. The new route begins at the Muskoka Heritage Park in Huntsville, where a new two-storey station houses a waiting room, ticket office and historic photos, as well as community meeting rooms on the second floor. The trains now follow a 1.25-kilometre route along the banks of the Muskoka River to the shore of Fairy Lake, where the purser's cabin from the dock of a nearby hotel on Fairy Lake has become the Fairy Lake "station." To house the heritage rolling stock, the volunteers erected an engine shed and 500 metres of siding. The station is located on Brunel Street in Huntsville.

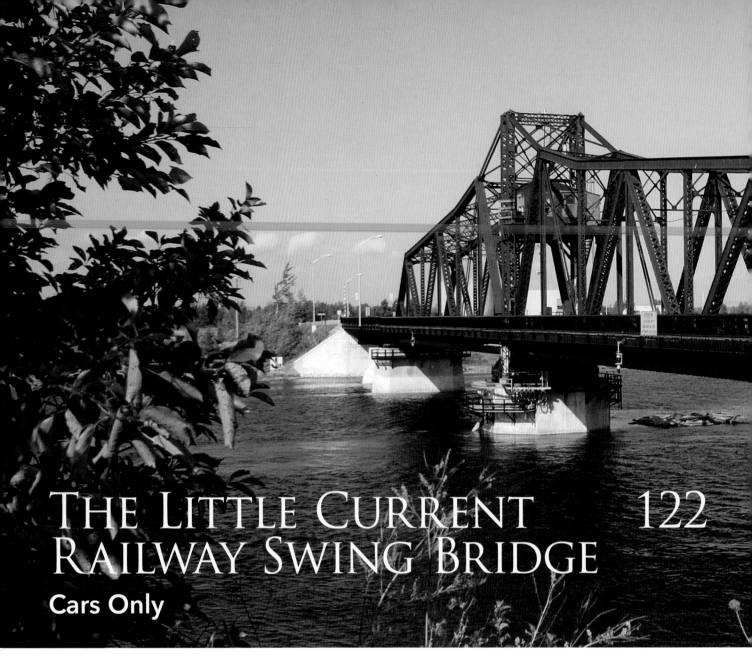

THE LITTLE CURRENT RAILWAY SWING BRIDGE   122
Cars Only

ONE OF ONTARIO's more interesting anomalies is that the only road access to the world's largest freshwater island is via a railway bridge.

Since the end of the last ice age, Manitoulin Island was considered a sacred place for its Aboriginal populations. Europeans began to drive those inhabitants from their land in the 1860s, and within a few years most of that land was in the hands of the settlers.

For several decades the "Haweaters," as the Manitoulin pioneers called themselves (for their dependence on the local hawberry), depended on water crossings to link them with the mainland. Then in 1893, the Algoma Eastern Railway began building a track from Sudbury to the island with the idea that its line would eventually link up with a line to Tobermory on the tip of the Bruce Peninsula. But, as with many a railway dream, the plan fell short, terminating instead at the island port of Little Current.

To span the gap between the mainland and the island, a long bridge was needed— one that would also allow the passage of the busy steamship traffic of the North Channel.

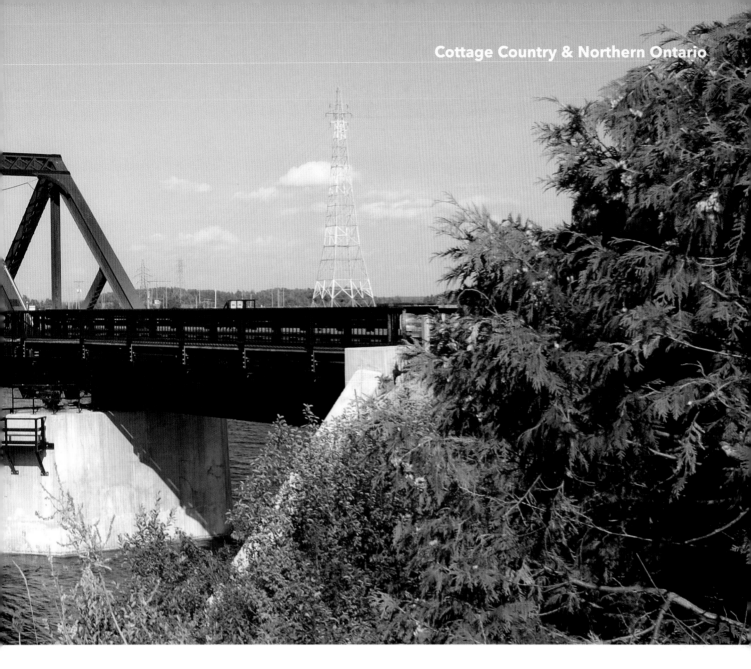

The only vehicular access to the world's largest freshwater island, Manitoulin, is via a century-old railway swing bridge.

In 1913, the bridge opened to train traffic. At 225 metres long it contains a 112-metre span, which swings open and allow ships to pass. Until 1946 it served rail only, with all other traffic using a nearby ferry. In those days it remained open until a train arrived. Since 1946, however, when vehicles began to share it, the bridge has remained in the closed position, opening during the ice-free season for fifteen minutes out of every hour to allow boat traffic through.

Finally, in the 1980s, train service was cut back and the bridge planked in. Today the entire rail line has been abandoned. Although cars may also use the ferry *Chi-Cheemaun* between Tobermory and South Baymouth, it is the old railway swing bridge that remains the iconic symbol of the island, while hawberry jelly has become a popular souvenir gift item.

The bridge forms part of Highway 6 south of Espanola.

ONTARIO'S STONEHENGE

THE LARDER LAKE area of Ontario was one of the more significant spiritual centres for Ontario's early Aboriginal populations. Important early canoe routes made their way from the Ottawa River and Lake Temiskaming systems and mounted a height of land before making their way through the Abitibi and Moose River systems and on to James Bay.

Along the way, the most prominent feature is a looming cylindrical volcanic rock plug known as Mount Cheminis. Its physical dominance made it a place of worship for the Ojibwas and Crees who passed through the water system. Many chose the height of land on which to build their villages. The route was also used by early explorers and fur traders as well as by Chevalier Pierre de Troyes, who in 1686 led a surprise commando-style raid on the British Moose Fort on the Moose River.

But the most unusual of the route's features is an arrangement of eighteen massive boulders on the north shore of Larder Lake. How did such gigantic rocks end up in the same place and in a distinctive arrangement? Recent investigations have revealed that the boulders are so configured that they line up with the sunrise and sunset at the times of the summer and winter solstices.

It is theorized, then, that the site represents a calendar used by early Aboriginal shamans about twelve hundred years ago. Its purpose would be similar to that of the stones used by the Druid worshippers at Stonehenge on the Salisbury Plain of England. Similar too would be the challenge in positioning boulders that, in some instances, are three times the height of the people who would have moved them. Such a focus would also be consistent with the use of Mount Cheminis as a place for spiritual worship.

The rocks are located near Pearl Beach on Larder Lake, east of the town of the same name.

123

Massive boulders near Larder Lake may have served a calendar-type purpose similar to that of the Stonehenge circle in England.

A TOUCH OF ASIA
The Thunder Bay Pagoda

FOR MANY DECADES, it was the first thing visitors to Port Arthur would see. As they disembarked from a CP steamship, or a train at the CPR station, visitors would make this unusual tourist information centre their first stop. Situated by the harbour and the tracks and on the walk to the Prince Arthur Hotel, Port Arthur's "publicity pagoda" was built in 1909. Given Port Arthur's harsh climate of long, bitterly cold winters and uncompromising terrain, civic leaders and the business community desperately needed something to enhance their town's appeal. After all, the new Prince Arthur Hotel was slated to open in 1910, and the town was anxious for a visual icon to counter rival Fort William, by then a major transportation hub.

And so the town leaders hired a local architect named H. Russell Halton to create what has become Ontario's most unusual tourist pavilion. Octagonal in shape, the brick and stone pavilion is topped with a Hindu-style chatri roof, with Tuscan-like columns supporting a veranda around it. The local culture is represented by a bas-relief beaver and maple leaf carvings above the French-door entrance. At the time, the pavillion was known as the "publicity pagoda"—notion being to create an "east-west" concept to make all visitors feel welcome.

By the mid-1980s, rail passenger service had dwindled and ultimately ended altogether. The CPR station was demolished and the pagoda moved inland to accommodate new roadways along the waterfront. Although it survived a period during the 1970s with a polka-dotted roof, in 1986 the office closed and the pagoda appeared doomed. In an effort to save the structure, the federal government declared it a national historic site. Fortunately, in 1988, the city, which in 1970 had become Thunder Bay with the amalgamation of Port Arthur and Fort William, received a Heritage grant and restoration began.

Today, the remarkable pagoda still stands—the Prince Arthur Hotel on one side and the stunning Canadian Northern railway station, with its twin pyramid roofs, on the other. It is considered Canada's oldest information office. Happily, the polka dots are now gone.

124

As it has for more than a century, Thunder Bay's unusual pagoda-style
information booth welcomes visitors to what was downtown Port Arthur.

125

Pictographs on Lake Superior depict early Native omens and myths.

STORIES ON THE ROCK
The Agawa Pictographs

A SHEER GRANITE WALL assailed by the crashing waves of Lake Superior would be the last place one would look to find Aboriginal stories, but here in Lake Superior Provincial Park are some of the best preserved pictographs anywhere in Canada.

Pictographs are quite different from petroglyphs, such as those found near Stony Lake, which are carvings. Pictographs are paintings. Made of mixtures of red ochre and animal fat, the images are surprisingly durable. Those on the Agawa rock wall may date back more than three centuries.

Here, on the sheer 30-metre rock face, nearly three dozen images portray what is said to be a victory battle by a party of Ojibwa over invading Iroquois. Following the devastating raids by the Iroquois against the Hurons in the mid-seventeenth century, groups of Ojibwa warriors retaliated, driving many of the invaders back across the Great Lakes and into their home territory of upper New York State.

Rediscovered in 1958, the images appear in four panels (three of which are accessible), the main one depicting a pair of large snakes and a great lynx guarding a canoe of Ojibwa fighters. According to Native lore, the lynx is the protector of the Ojibwa. Other panels portray other animals, including an eagle, a beaver and a heron, purported to represent different clans. The presence of a horse suggests that the drawings were done post-contact with Europeans.

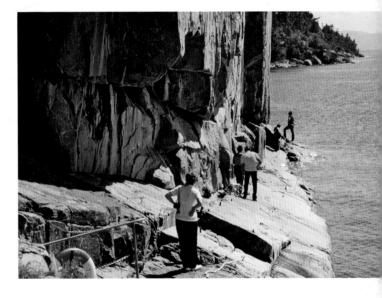

A 400-metre trail leads down through a narrow defile in the rock to the site. Because access is only via a narrow ledge along the lake, visits should not be attempted in stormy weather. An unusual sight along the trail itself is a huge boulder wedged solidly between narrow canyon walls high above the trail. The park straddles Highway 17, south of Wawa.

Above: Visiting the exposed Agawa pictographs on Lake Superior is off-limits during rough weather on the lake.

INDEX

Index

Answer to the Bean Cryptogram

Starting with the letter "I," read in a zig-zag counter-clockwise direction and the following dedication appears:

"In memoriam Henrietta, 1st wife of S. Bean. M.D. who died 27th Sep 1865 aged 23 years 2 months and 17 days & Susanna his second wife who died 27th April 1867 aged 26 years 3 months and 15 days.

"2 better wives 1 man never had. They were gifts from God and are now in Heaven. May God help me S.B. to meet them there."